THE Day Trader's Survival Guide

Also by Christopher A. Farrell

Day Trade Online

CHRISTOPHER A. FARRELL

THE Day Trader's Survival Guide

How to Be Consistently Profitable in Short-Term Markets

HarperBusiness
An Imprint of HarperColllins*Publishers*

The section of chapter 7 entitled "Playing the Specialist's Game" (p. 152) first appeared in the May 2000 issue of *Active Trader* magazine and is reprinted with permission.

While the methods of investment described in this book are believed to be effective, there is no guarantee that the method will be profitable in specific applications, owing to the risk that is involved in investing of almost any kind. Thus neither the publisher nor the author assume liability for any losses that may be sustained by the use of the methods described in this book, and any such liability is hereby expressly disclaimed.

FIRST EDITION

Library of Congress Cataloging-in-Publication Data

Farrell, Christopher, A., 1973–
    The day trader's survival guide : how to be consistently profitable in short-term markets / Christopher A. Farrell.—1st ed.
        p. cm.
    ISBN 0-06-662085-6
    1. Electronic trading of securities. I. Title.

  HG4515.95 .F368 2000
  332.64'0285—dc21

                                                                    00-040742

00   01   02   03   04   QF   10   9   8   7   6   5   4   3   2   1

To my father,
Robert J. Farrell,
For Being There,
Always

Be prepared to suffer severe financial losses.

—Arthur Levitt, chairman,
Securities and Exchange Commission

Contents

Preface

THE SUCKER

There is an old saying in gambling,
That when you sit down at the poker table,
Expecting to take everyone else's money,
Of all the players sitting around you,
If within five minutes,
You can't tell who the sucker is,
Then chances are,
The sucker is you

In this day and age, successful day trading is about surviving lightning fast market movements, bad executions, the unfair and unscrupulous practices of the Wall Street trading firms, and, last but not least, surviving the ridiculous stereotypes and misinformation about day traders that exist. I am excited about this book because it says many of the things about Wall Street—and about day trading—that other people have been afraid to say.

I'm sure many of you have read the horror stories in the media about investors who have lost their life savings after they "dabbled" in day trading. Many individuals enter the day trading arena with the intention of making a quick killing, and instead the market teaches them a harsh lesson and they leave the arena penniless. In fact, there have been industry reports that say that as many as seven out of every ten day traders ultimately lose money. But not everyone loses money. Some make a very good living, and there are a privileged few—many in their early twenties—who have been able to make six- and seven figure salaries year after year.

Aside from Hollywood, Silicon Valley, and professional sports, successful day traders can make more money in a shorter space of time than they can in any other profession. So what, exactly, is it about the short-term mechanics of the market that prevents so many day traders from being profitable? What is this mysterious "market force" that has claimed the life savings of so many novice day traders yet is also capable of producing incredible riches for a lucky few who can harness its power? This book is intended to answer that very question.

One of the early mistakes that many novice day traders make is that they get caught up in the hype of the online trading revolution. Technology is advancing at a faster clip every single day, but don't believe the ads you see on television. Just because you can get a trade executed in a split second with the click of a mouse, that does *not* mean that you are on a level playing field with the rest of Wall Street.

If most day traders lose money, it logically follows that someone is making money at their expense. If you lose $25,000 playing the market, the money doesn't just vanish into thin air. So what are all of these day traders doing wrong, and why are they always on the losing side? How come those few day traders who are successful end up with all of their money? Consider this: Do seven out of ten Wall Street trading firms lose money? Do Goldman Sachs, Morgan Stanley, First Boston, and Merrill Lynch consistently lose money? Absolutely not! They make money hand over fist, year in and year out. This merely proves that there is a way to exploit this system for profit, and it involves beating Wall Street at its own game.

From this point forward, take everything that you ever learned about investing and forget it. The first thing that the day trader must understand is that in the short term stocks act quite differently than they do over the long term. The techniques that apply to long-term investing *do not* work in the short term. If you approach day trading the same way that you approach investing, you are sure to lose money.

You will learn many things in this book that you have never known before. There are cutting-edge trading strategies mentioned here that you will never see in any other books written on day trading or online trading. My intention in writing this book is not to sell you on the dream of quitting your job and trading for a living. Instead, we will take the high road.

This book will show you how it is done. Remember, all of Wall Street is out to take your money. This book will show you how to take their money instead.

Note to reader: If you have any questions about the subject matter in this book, you can contact me at my website: *www.farrell trading.com.*

Acknowledgments

On a professional note, I must thank all of the great people at HarperBusiness, especially my editor, David Conti, and his assistants, Devi Pillai and Eula Biss, for their help and hard work in making this book a reality.

In addition, I must thank my parents, my brother, Peter, and all of my extended family, my friends, and my fellow traders for their help, support, and inspiration.

Introduction
Wall Street's Virtual Casino

Wall Street and Las Vegas have much in common. While Las Vegas has blackjack dealers and croupiers, Wall Street has market makers, specialists, and online brokers. And, just like the casinos, Wall Street exists for one and only one reason: to take your money as quickly as possible.

Open Season on Day Traders

There are only two certainties in the financial world: Wall Street will always make money at the expense of the investing public, and day traders will always be hated. As you may know, only in the last several years has online trading and day trading taken hold. But the animosity toward day traders is higher today than ever before. The incredible advances in the Internet and in trading technology have completely changed the landscape of Wall Street, and day trading has been the engine behind much of it. Just think about what you can do from the comfort of your own home that you couldn't do five years ago: You can place trades, get real-time quotes, and, most important, you can participate and exploit market movements as they are happening. The closed world ruled by the world's largest financial institutions is now open to anyone with a small amount of capital, a computer, and Internet access. The "little guy" has finally been let into the club. And, despite what it says, traditional Wall Street still doesn't like it one bit.

The Unwelcome Guest at Wall Street's Feast

Over the last three years, the proliferation of day trading into every segment of the equity markets has become a serious and formidable threat to Wall Street's profits. When a day trader is successful, it is because he extracts profits from the market that are normally reserved for the institutional traders and brokerage firms. Every dollar a day trader makes is one less dollar for Wall Street.

> **"This electronic access has created an opportunity for the day traders . . . who are not my favorite people."**
>
> **—MURIEL SIEBERT**
> *President of online broker Muriel Siebert and Co.*
> *September 22, 1999*

The Short-Term Mechanics of the Market Have Been Put Under the Magnifying Glass

Five years ago the best and most profitable firms on Wall Street had a virtual monopoly on trading profits. The only direct competition they faced was from other "member" firms, and there were no outsiders. But one of the consequences of the advance in technology has been the fact that for the first time in history, the short-term mechanics of the market have been placed under a magnifying glass. The investing public has begun to witness at firsthand just how lucrative the short-term movements of the market can be, and just how much money Wall Street has been making at its expense all these years. So the one area of the market that was kept shrouded in secrecy by the Wall Street trading firms is no longer a secret. Technology has opened the door, and the day trader has stepped in. And that is where we stand today.

Is the Playing Field Really Level?

In the last couple of years it has often been said that these changes in technology have "leveled the playing field" for the individual investor. But the fact that so many day traders still lose money even in light of these changes stands as evidence that the playing field is really not level. The reason so many lose when trying to play the short-term movements of the market is quite simple: *Wall Street will do everything in its power to prevent the day trader from being profitable.* But how does it accomplish this, and what does it do to consistently fool the majority of day traders? To begin to answer this question, we need to look at precisely how the short-term mechanics of the market work, and the ways in which Wall Street makes its money within this system.

Wall Street Has Always Been Ahead of the Curve

No matter how hard the investing public tries, they always seem to be one step behind Wall Street. Think about the last time you bought a "hot stock" that was "guaranteed" to go higher, yet right after you bought it, it dropped like a rock. How about the time you were going to double your money on a quick trade, only to have your trading capital cut in half instead? These kinds of things happen all the time, and they are no accident. *When Wall Street is involved, there is no such thing as easy money.* No matter how great the prospects for making money may look, there is always someone taking the other side of your trade. Remember, every buyer has a seller, and there is a very good chance that the person taking the other side of your trade knows more than you do about where the stock is headed.

Look at your classic panic-sell situation. What happens when the investing public is recklessly dumping a stock? Who is there to buy it from them when they all rush for the exits at the same time? And, even worse, when the stock is so "hot" that buyers will pay any price to get their hands on it, who is there to sell it to them? As you know, it is the Wall Street trading firms.

The Investing Public's Entry into a Stock Is Usually Wall Street's Exit

This is an ironic situation. When the stock is up 30 points on the day and looks as if it is headed higher, Wall Street is actually selling, and when the stock is down 30 points on the day and looks as if it is going lower, these financial institutions are probably buying. While the banks and brokerage firms use rallies as an opportunity to sell stock, and dips as an opportunity to buy stock, the investing public does the opposite. That is what we mean when we say that these trading firms stay ahead of the curve by doing the exact opposite of what the public thinks they are doing: They buy stock when no one wants it, and they sell it when everyone wants it. In other words, the public's entry into a stock is Wall Street's exit. The result? *Wall Street consistently makes money while the investing public loses it.*

If it is true that Wall Street usually makes money and the investing public usually loses it, on whose side of the trade would you rather be? If you can be on the same side of the trade as Wall Street, if you can buy when they are buying, and sell when they are selling, don't the odds say that over time you will make money? The answer is yes. This sheds light on one of the most important yet misunderstood principles of day trading: *The most successful day traders make money not because they trade against the Wall Street firms but because they trade with them.* This is the blueprint that any beginning day trader must follow if he or she expects to survive and prosper in this game.

At face value it would seem very difficult for Wall Street to consistently "fake out" the investing public. The general public is not stupid and, in fact, they are more sophisticated today than ever before. But still it seems that when they get involved in short-term trading, they always end up on the short end of the stick. So what is the secret? What does Wall Street have that the general public doesn't? Wall Street has a very easy way of getting the investing public's money, and it has nothing to do with studying charts or combing through piles of research on a company.

Making money on Wall Street is much easier than that. The Street designed a system that effectively allows them to "siphon" money from their customers' pockets every single time they place a trade. This is an age-old vehicle on Wall Street, but it has only been recently that the public has begun to understand how it works, and how it has been used against them. The mechanism is called the bid-ask spread.

THE BID-ASK SPREAD: THE MACHINE THAT SIPHONS THE INVESTING PUBLIC'S MONEY INTO THE HANDS OF WALL STREET

How is Wall Street's money-making machine able to siphon money from the investing public each and every trading day?

EXODUS COMMUNICATIONS

(EXDS)
$138\frac{1}{8}$ to $138\frac{7}{8}$
$138\frac{1}{8}$ bid, offered at $138\frac{7}{8}$

Wall Street is able to "print money" day in and day out, year in and year out because of the mechanism known as the bid-ask spread. In Exodus Communications, a NASDAQ stock, Wall Street is a buyer of stock at $138\frac{1}{8}$ and a seller of stock at $138\frac{7}{8}$.

Bid	Ask
$138\frac{1}{8}$	$138\frac{7}{8}$
Wall Street Buys	Wall Street Sells
Investing Public Sells	Investing Public Buys

Wall Street attempts to pocket "the spread," or the difference between the bid price and the ask price, which in this example is ¾ of a point. This means that regardless of whether the stock goes higher or lower, the large brokerage firms can "scalp" ¾ point, or $0.75 per share, at the expense of the buying and selling of the investing public. If the stock trades several million shares per day, Wall Street can accumulate hundreds of millions of dollars per year trading this way. *The only reason the market maker is willing to buy stock at 138⅛ is because it is almost certain that it can turn right around and sell it at a higher price (138⅞).*

The Bid-Ask Spread Is Wall Street's Gold Mine

Imagine two investors who simultaneously place orders. One has to sell 2,000 shares of EXDS, while another has to buy 2,000 shares. In a perfect world the brokerage firm would "match" the orders and give both buyer and seller the same price. But Wall Street is not a perfect world. The brokerage firm will instead "gouge" the customers, buying 2,000 at 138⅛ from customer A and selling 2,000 to customer B at 138⅞. The brokerage firm will pocket $1,500 *completely at the expense of its customers.*

The only reason these market makers are in business in the first place is to make the spread. They risk their own capital all day long in the attempt to take ¹⁄₁₆ths, ⅛ths, ¼s, and ½s out of the market. *In other words, the market makers are in the business of trading against their customers.*

The Bid-Ask Spread Is the Reason for Online Trades Being So Cheap!

If you have any doubts as to just how lucrative the game of making the spread can be, you need look no farther than the online brokers themselves for assurance. Why do the online brokers charge only $10, $8, or even $5 per trade up to 5,000 shares? How can they make any money on the $5 commission for 5,000 shares? If you went back ten years, do you know how much a 5,000-share trade would cost you at a full-service broker? Thousands of dollars. Back then, the investing public had absolutely no idea how much money the full-service brokerage firms were making at their expense. But the landscape of Wall Street changed when online trading took hold. The "fat cats" were getting priced right out of business. As a result, over a series of years, the full-service brokerage firms went from a $3,000 commission, in some cases, down to as low as $19.95! And, as you know, in this day and age the online brokers are even cheaper than that. Some charge only $10 or less.

So what's the catch? How could a brokerage firm go from charging $3,000 to charging $19.95 and still make money? And even worse, how can an online broker who charges only $5 for a 5,000-share trade possibly stay in business? The answer is that the online brokers don't make their money on the $5 commission, but *on the trade itself*. In other words, they profit from the bid-ask spread. Though it may not seem so at first glance, the game of "making the spread" is a very profitable enterprise. In fact, it is so lucrative that some trading firms on Wall Street actually "purchase" order flow from online brokers just for the chance to pocket the spread on your trades. This practice is called "payment for order flow." (See chapter 2.)

To give you an idea of just how lucrative the business of making the spread can be, let's look at another example. Imagine placing an order to buy 5,000 shares of EXDS through your online broker. You bought it, got nervous, and turned right around and sold it seconds later. If the stock didn't move between the time you bought it and sold it, before commissions you will have broken even on the trade, right? WRONG! Even though the stock didn't budge, you will still have lost almost $4,000! You bought 5,000 shares at 138⅞ (the ask) and sold at 138⅛ (the bid) and lost $3,750 on a stock that didn't budge! The online broker made almost $4,000 at your expense. That is why they charge you only $5 for the trade.

EASY MONEY: A $5,000 PROFIT FOR LESS THAN TWO SECONDS OF WORK

The ideal situation for any Wall Street trading desk is to have two "offsetting" customer orders in hand.

VERT   210–211

1. Brokerage firm simultaneously buys 5,000 from customer A at 210.

2. While it sells 5,000 to customer B at 211.

A 5,000-share buy order and a 5,000-share sell order will not be "matched." Instead, when bid-ask spreads are $1 wide, the brokerage firm will buy 5,000 from customer A at 210 and immediately resell 5,000 to customer B at 211, resulting in a $5,000 profit with virtually no risk for the trading desk.

Is This Profit Justified?

Wall Street would argue that the $5,000 profit made here was justified, because the trading desk was exposed to a substantial amount of market risk by committing trading capital. In theory, anyone who buys 5,000 shares of VERT is taking a large risk, because the stock can move 2 or 3 points in a matter of seconds. However, in this case there was no risk and no outlay of trading capital because the trades were "laid off." In other words, you had the buyer and seller lined up at the same time. *The trading desk was never at risk of losing money.* Do you think the customers knew that? Do you think the brokerage firm would tell them? These are the kinds of trades Wall Street loves.

Like the free comps at a casino, the cheap cost of online trades is nothing more than a gimmick to "lure" investors into trading against the online brokerage firms, in the hope that the online broker can profit from the bid-ask spread at the customer's expense.

The Dealer's Side of the Blackjack Table

The day trader must view the bid-ask spread in the same way you would approach a blackjack or a craps table at a Las Vegas casino. Who are the winners and how do they win? Who rakes in the money when the "suckers" are losing it? The sad truth about the casino is that despite the riches they promise, the only consistent winner is the house—the guy on the dealer's side of the table. The casino likes to make the dealer's edge seem so slight and inconspicuous that the gambling patrons have no idea just how slim the odds are of taking the casino's money. In other words, the typical gambler really has no idea just how much of a "sucker" he really is. The same is true of the typical online investor.

Beating Them at Their Own Game

So what is Wall Street's equivalent of being on the dealer's side of a blackjack table, and how can the day trader get involved? It is very simple. The day trader can beat the online brokerage firms at their own game by attempting to "make" the spread instead of "paying" the spread. By doing so the day trader puts the odds of making a profit in his favor. However, it is not as easy as it looks.

Before the day trader can go out and exploit the markets, he or she must have a firm understanding of how the system works. At the heart of this is knowing the critical difference between market and limit orders. When an investor enters a "market" order, he is agreeing to pay the spread. In other words, if it is a buy order "at market," the investor agrees to buy stock at whatever price the market makers have stock for sale, no matter how high. Market orders are the easiest way to lose money.

Who's the Sucker?

Remember the sucker theme from the preface? On Wall Street, who's the sucker? The sucker is the person who uses "market orders," who pays the spread on every trade. The sucker overpays on the way in and gets underpaid on the way out.

DCLK   120–120¼
120 bid, offered at 120¼

The active trader cannot afford to pay the spread on every trade. In the above example, if you traded 10,000 shares of DCLK during the day, and paid the spread on every trade, you would be leaving $2,500 on the table. That $2,500 is pure profit in the pocket of the market maker who was able to capture it. *If you use market orders, and pay the spread on every trade, it will be impossible to make a living as a day trader.*

When Using Market Orders, Think of the "Sucking Sound" of a Vacuum Cleaner

If you are tempted to use market orders, just imagine the sound of a vacuum cleaner every time you use one. The "sucking sound" you hear is money being sucked out of your wallet by the Wall Street trading firms. In fact, by using market orders, so much money is being sucked out of your wallet that the odds of a profitable trade could be as low as one in five.

PHCM   135–136

If you are buying and selling PHCM "at market," the stock has to move a full point in your direction, not to make money but just for you to break even! If it doesn't move, you are a guaranteed loser. You will be buying at 136 (the ask) and selling at 135 (the bid), and losing 1 full point on a trade that, on paper, didn't go against you.

PAYING THE SPREAD IS A DOUBLE WHAMMY: IT MINIMIZES YOUR GAINS WHILE EXAGGERATING YOUR LOSSES

If the PHCM stock drops 1 measly point, the day trader who uses market orders will not have lost just 1 point. By paying the spread, he or she will actually have lost 2 full points! The day trader will have bought stock at 136 and sold stock at 134, losing 2 points on a stock that only dropped 1. This is the problem with market orders.

PHCM   135–136

becomes . . .

PHCM   134–135

The spread exaggerates your losses and minimizes your gains! Any day trader who relies upon the use of "market orders" will be out of business in a very short period of time.

The Ability to "Capture" the Spread Rests Upon the Use of Limit Orders

So if the "sucker" was using market orders and losing money on the trade, who was making money? Who made $2 per share when the day trader lost it? It was the Wall Street trading firm using limit orders to take the other side of these trades! When the day trader bought stock at 136 and sold at 134, someone else bought at 134 and sold at 136. While the day trader lost $2 by paying the spread, someone else made $2 by making the spread. Imagine how this "edge" is magnified if you do several thousand trades per year. This mechanism is exactly what causes seven out of ten day traders to lose money. *Paying the spread on every trade is Wall Street's equivalent of going to the casino, and consistently betting against the house.* You may get lucky in the short term, but over time, if you do this long enough, you will eventually be out of business. This is the fine line between making a very good living and going broke on Wall Street.

The Limit Order Undermines Wall Street's Ability to Make the Spread

If using a market order is a bet *against* the house, it can be said that the use of a limit order is a bet *with* the house. This is why day traders who use limit orders have a much higher survival rate. A limit order, unlike a market order, allows the investor to put a price limit on how much he or she will pay for the stock. *The essence of using a limit order lies in the fact that it allows you to buy stock at a lower price than where it is for sale, and, in the process, to undermine Wall Street.* How is it possible to do this? Let's look at an example.

AOL   **60–60⅜**

As the quote for America Online shows, stock is for sale at 60⅜. If the day trader is smart, he will not attempt to buy stock at 60⅜. Why not? Because paying 60⅜ for stock is a bet against the house! In other words, the odds of turning a profit after buying it at 60⅜ are not with you, they are against you. Savvy day traders would actually be looking to sell stock at 60⅜, not buy it there.

With this in mind, the day trader will try to buy it for less, perhaps at 60, 60¹⁄₁₆, or 60⅛—price levels where the odds of a profitable trade are much higher. If the trader enters a buy order for 1,000 shares on a 60⅛ limit, he is saying that he will pay 60⅛ for 1,000 shares and not a penny higher.

AOL   **60⅛–60⅜**

If the day trader is skillful enough to buy stock at 60⅛, he will have saved $250 on the trade, buying stock ¼ point cheaper than where the Wall Street trading firm had the stock for sale (60⅜). In addition to saving money on the way in, the day trader also sets himself up to make a nice profit on the trade. In this example, the odds of selling the stock for a small profit at 60¼, 60⁵⁄₁₆, or 60⅜ are good. This is why we say that the use of limit orders undermines Wall Street. It allows the day trader to do the same thing to the stock that the large trading firms do: *to make the spread as opposed to paying it.*

Shouldn't Wall Street Love Day Traders Who Consistently Lose Money?

Hopefully, you are now beginning to see how Wall Street is able to make so much money at the expense of the investing public. But if Wall Street profits at the individual investor's expense, doesn't it also profit at the expense of the seven out of the ten day traders who lose money on every trade? The answer is yes. The day traders are as much "the sucker" as the investing public. But what about the other three out of ten day traders who consistently make money? In contrast, the minority of successful day traders are by no means considered "suckers" in the eyes of Wall Street. In fact, they are actually feared by the establishment. They are disliked because, as a group, these day traders have undermined the Wall Street money-making machine. In the process, these day traders have hit Wall Street where it hurts most—in the wallet.

Wall Street Will Take You to the Cleaners If You Rely Upon Fundamentals

This is as good a place as any to drive home one of the major themes of the book: If you are a day trader (as opposed to a long-term investor), and you rely upon charts, graphs, and research to guide you, Wall Street will take you to the cleaners. I hate to keep using the term "sucker," but the novice trader who combs through piles of market research, brokerage recommendations, and price charts is perhaps the biggest "sucker" of all. Why? Because he is basing his buy and sell decisions on false and misleading barometers of supply and demand. The information the day trader needs to turn a profit in the next few seconds can never be found in the "fundamentals"—the charts, balance sheets, and research reports that so many investors rely upon.

> *No matter how "bullish" a price chart may look, or how glowing an analyst's recommendation sounds, the day trader who ignores the bid-ask spread will not last in this business.*

No matter how many hours you spend researching a stock, talking to analysts, and watching CNBC, if you pay the spread on the trade, you will completely nullify any advantage that you thought you had over the rest of the trading community. Think about it. What good does a brokerage firm's research report do you if you are down ½ point because you didn't know the difference between a market order and a limit order?

HOW PRICE CHARTS AND MARKET RESEARCH CAN FOOL YOU

Though the price chart and a buy recommendation from Goldman Sachs may make Celera Genomics (CRA) look like a good investment, this is a guaranteed loser from the day trader's standpoint. With a bid-ask spread that is 2 points wide, any day trader who buys CRA (CRA) "at market" is out $2 per share before he even begins!

CRA   77–79

What chance does the trader possibly have of turning a profit if, on paper, he is immediately down 2 points the second he buys the stock? Yes, a loser from the start. But the charts, graphs, and research won't tell you that—exactly the way that Wall Street intended it.

The Wider the Spreads, the More Profit for Wall Street

The Wall Street trading firms have a vested financial interest in keeping bid-ask spreads as wide as possible, even if it is unfair to the investing public. The wider the spreads, the harder it is for the investing public to come out on the winning side of the trade. Thus the wider the spreads, the more profit for Wall Street.

The day trading revolution has put Wall Street in a very peculiar position. It obviously wants to keep the bid-ask spreads as wide as is humanly possible, to make it easy to profit at the expense of the investing public. However, it can no longer do this effectively without getting undercut by the very day traders it is trying to trade against. The consequence of keeping bid-ask spreads unfairly wide is to leave the door wide open for the day traders like you and me to step through in front of them. This is the risk that Wall Street runs by getting greedy in an age when it is not the only one who can watch and exploit the short-term movements of the market.

The Online Trading Revolution Has Narrowed Spreads

A consequence of this is that the more the day trading revolution has taken hold, the more narrow the bid-ask spreads have become. This has actually benefited the investing public, but has, in the process, undercut Wall Street's profit margins. As we have said before, Wall Street would like to keep the spreads as wide as possible, even if the investing public is getting ripped off.

The Mechanics of Price Movement

Now that we have had a brief introduction to the mechanics of the bid-ask spread, we need to delve deeper into the phenomenon known as price movement. What is it that makes a stock go higher or lower? At face value, this is a very simple question. Yet I bet if you asked ten different "experts" on Wall Street, you'd get ten different answers. The superficial explanation is, obviously, that buyers and sellers move markets. Supply and demand imbalances move the market higher or lower. This leads me to believe that the question that is so hard to answer is not *why* a stock moves higher or lower, but *how* a stock moves higher or lower. Let's look at an example.

How Does a Stock Move Higher?

A stock moves higher because there is only a limited amount of it for sale at each price level. Once all of the stock at a given price level is "cleaned out," the next buyer will be forced to pay a higher price to buy the stock. Here is how Office Depot (ODP) can move up $\frac{1}{8}$ point in a matter of seconds:

1st phase: ODP $\quad\quad\quad 14\frac{3}{8}–14\frac{1}{2} \quad\quad\quad 1,000 \times 1,000$

An investor wants to buy 4,000 shares "at market." Here's what happens:

1. He immediately buys 1,000 shares at $14\frac{1}{2}$, and Wall Street updates the ask:

2nd phase: $\quad\quad\quad\quad 14\frac{3}{8}–14\frac{9}{16} \quad\quad\quad 1,000 \times 1,000$

2. Investor is filled on another 1,000 share lot, this time at $14\frac{9}{16}$, and the market updates:

3rd phase: $\quad\quad\quad\quad 14\frac{3}{8}–14\frac{5}{8} \quad\quad\quad 1,000 \times 2,000$

3. Investor completes the order by buying the remaining 2,000 shares at $14\frac{5}{8}$. It took only one buyer of 4,000 shares to cause ODP to tick up $\frac{1}{8}$th point. The investor was unable to buy all 4,000 shares at $14\frac{1}{2}$ because there was simply not enough stock for sale at that level. Supply and demand forced him to "pay up" to accumulate stock.

Understanding how this mechanism works will become very important in later chapters. The most successful day traders all share an ability to read and understand the mechanics of price movement. Are buyers lifting offers, or are sellers hitting bids? Are large blocks of stock trading at the bid, or at the offer? Is there one large seller who is driving the stock down? These are all questions that the day trader asks himself throughout the trading day. If you can't read these movements, how are you going to be able to exploit them? By the time you have finished this book, you should have a good knowledge of how these movements work.

On Wall Street, What a Stock Is Really "Worth" Is Inconsequential

In the eyes of Wall Street, what is a stock really worth? You may be surprised to know that no one on Wall Street really cares. A stock is worth only what someone else is willing to pay for it. *And to Wall Street, the stock is worth only slightly less than at what price it can be sold.* That is the only valuation that the banks and brokerage firms are concerned with. For instance, if it can be sold at 100, then to Wall Street it is probably "worth" 99¾. And if it can be sold for only 8, then to a trader it is "worth" only 7⅞. This is something the day trader must understand: In the game of supply and demand, absolute value has no meaning.

The Million-Dollar Question: Isn't It More Economical to Just Buy and Hold?

Many people skeptical of day trading have asked this question: Isn't it better to just buy and hold than to compulsively buy and sell all day long? On a day when a momentum stock like Rambus goes from $210 to $260, wouldn't it be better to just buy the stock in the morning at $210 and sell it at the end of the day at $260 instead of getting in and out twenty times? No, and here is my reasoning. How do you know that when the stock is trading at $210, it is going to end up later that day at $260? Doesn't it have just as much chance of going to $160? The point is, no one knows what the market is going to do, not even the brightest minds on Wall Street. If everyone knew that the stock would end the day at $260, why was it trading at $210 in the first place?

You are far better off limiting your risk and scalping high percentage ½s and points than buying and holding. What if the stock goes from 210 to 220, but then ends up later that day at 160? While the buy and hold investor is "married" to the stock as it is tanking, the day trader is either out of his position entirely, or short the stock. The successful day trader probably made money on the way up on the long side, and then also made money on the way down on the short side.

Remember, the day trader is not concerned with picking perfect tops and bottoms. All he is looking to do is take chunks of profits out of the larger movements. Quarter points, half points, and points on the way up, quarters and halves and points on the way down, and sixteenths and eighths when the stock doesn't move.

Is Day Trading Gambling?

In this chapter we have drawn many analogies between how Wall Street rips off the investing public and how the casinos gouge their gambling patrons. With that said, is day trading gambling? To answer this, compare the number of people you know who legitimately make a living from short-term investing with those who make a living from day trading. Successful day traders are a dime a dozen, yet you would be hard pressed to find anyone, other than the wealthiest Americans, who lives and dies by the value of his or her investment portfolio. And I don't mean the millions of people who actively follow the market with their mutual funds. I mean people who rely month after month solely on the money that their stock investments make them. I can't think of one single person who does because, over time, it is next to impossible to do this successfully.

Furthermore, if there was the slightest chance that it could be done successfully, don't you think Wall Street would be doing it already? Wouldn't it be far easier for Goldman Sachs, Morgan Stanley, or Merrill Lynch to "scrap" their entire market-making and trading operations, lay off the hundreds of highly paid traders, and simply invest the firm's billions of dollars of trading capital in the stock market instead? As you know, it wouldn't happen in a million years because the game of trading, specifically of "capturing the spread," is so much more of a lucrative and less risky business venture than the game of investing. The profits are almost guaranteed, year after year. In investing, as you know, they are not.

Investors Need a Bull Market to Make Money; Day Traders Do Not

To shed more light on this issue, think of the following situation. What happens to these so-called professional short-term investors in a year when the Dow Jones, the S&P 500, and the NASDAQ composite are flat? Can you still make a living as an investor if the market averages are in the toilet? The answer is no. Investors need a bull market to make money, day traders do not. Successful day traders can grind out a profit day in and day out, and they don't need the market to go higher to do it. So you tell me which one is gambling and which isn't.

Furthermore, in the process, the day trader's money is exposed to a much lower degree of "market risk." This is because the day trader is not trying to outsmart the market. Instead, he is simply exploiting the natural supply and demand imbalances that occur throughout the trading day. Like the rest of Wall Street, the successful day trader is a buyer when the market needs buyers, and a seller when the market needs sellers.

Are Goldman Sachs, Merrill Lynch, and Morgan Stanley Gamblers?

The message here is that anytime you are basing your buy and sell decisions on things outside the domain of the supply and demand in the stock, you are gambling. Wall Street doesn't gamble. But gambling is exactly what some short-term investors do when they act on a "hot" tip. These investors make buy and sell decisions outside the realm of supply and demand. In other words, they try to outsmart the market. Over time, that is extremely difficult to do, and it can be a recipe for failure. Think of how the most prestigious brokerage firms and banks on Wall Street make their money year in and year out. Would you call Goldman Sachs, Merrill Lynch, or Morgan Stanley gamblers? Do they make billions of dollars per year in trading profits because they "roll the dice"? Do their profits hinge on the market going higher? No, they don't. That is why successful day traders are not gamblers either.

Dispelling the Myth

I hope that I have begun to paint an accurate picture of how a successful day trader operates in a system designed to take his money away from him. I also hope that I have begun to dispel the myth that day traders are a bunch of reckless gamblers or "bandits" who wreak havoc on the markets in which they trade. Remember, successful day traders do not make their money by trading against the Wall Street brokerage firms. Anyone who tries to "pick off" the best and brightest traders on Wall Street is going to be out of the game very fast. Keep in mind that the house always wins. Like the casino, the consistent money on Wall Street is made by trading with the brokerage firms, not against them—in other words, by being on the dealer's side of the blackjack table, by betting *with* the house, not *against* it.

1

Wall Street's Money-Making Machine

Did you ever wonder what causes the NASDAQ market to be so much more volatile than the New York Stock Exchange? Would a NASDAQ stock like Qualcomm, which reached $800 per share in 1999, ever have traded that high under the NYSE's specialist system? No, it wouldn't have. What is it that is so different about the structure of NASDAQ that makes it so much more volatile, and potentially so much more profitable, than the NYSE? Why are those willing to take the highest risks inevitably drawn toward it? This chapter will answer those questions.

NASDAQ's Market-Maker System Is Much Different from the NYSE's Specialist System

The difference between the NASDAQ and the NYSE is like night and day. You need only look at the contrast in volatility between the two exchanges as evidence of this. When was the last time you saw a New York Stock Exchange stock swing 80 points between its high and its low in a single day? And when was the last time you saw an IPO on the NYSE open for trading 150 points higher than its offering price?

This never occurs on the NYSE. Yet gut-wrenching volatility happens every single day on the NASDAQ. IPOs priced at 20 that open at 200. Internet highfliers soar 1,000 percent in one trading day. Intra-day swings of 300 points in the NASDAQ composite index. This list goes on and on. So what causes the NASDAQ's incredible volatility?

Think back to April 14, 2000, the day the NASDAQ composite lost over 300 points. This was the culmination of one of the worst weeks in history, in which the NASDAQ composite lost almost 25 percent of its value. I remember looking at my quote screen in complete disbelief: Rambus (RMBS) was down over 46 points on the day, Redback (RBAK) had lost 26, and Brocade (BRCD) had lost 27. Yet if you glanced over at the New York Stock Exchange, which lost 600 points that day, the damage to individual stocks was not nearly as bad. Procter & Gamble (PG) was down 6, J. P. Morgan (JPM) lost 7, and General Motors (GM) lost 6. What is the reason for this discrepancy, and why did the NYSE seem to hold up better than NASDAQ during the panic selling?

Most people would conclude that the answer lies in the difference in the nature of the stocks that trade on the two exchanges. This is the easy answer. Seasoned and mature companies in the later stages of growth typify the New York Stock Exchange, companies like American Express, GE, and AT&T to name a few. High-flying Internet start-up companies, some with no earnings, characterize the domain of the NASDAQ. Included here would be "dot.com" bellwethers like Yahoo!, Amazon.com, and eBay. This contrast is partially to blame for the volatility. Naturally, a company like Amazon.com is going to have wider price swings than Ford. However, this is not the real reason for the volatility.

NASDAQ's Market-Maker System Is Inherently More Volatile Than the NYSE's Specialist System

There is no doubt that if you took the same stock and "listed it" on both the NASDAQ and the NYSE, it would experience a much higher degree of volatility on the NASDAQ. In other words, a 10-point move higher or lower in the stock's price on the NYSE could be a 20- or 30-point move in its price on the NASDAQ. This proves that it is not the stocks on the NASDAQ that cause the incredible volatility, but the system by which the stocks trade.

If the same stock traded under both the NYSE specialist system and the NASDAQ market-maker system, the stock would be inherently less volatile under the supervision of a specialist. The market makers don't share anywhere near the same level of "burden" to maintain an orderly market on NASDAQ as the specialist on the New York Stock Exchange.

The responsibility rests upon the group of NASDAQ market makers collectively, so each points a finger at one of the others when violations occur. The result? The market makers are less apt to support a falling stock, and even less inclined to contain a rising one. When the volatility gets completely out of control, it is the investing public who suffers the most. This is something that the NYSE loves to emphasize when comparing itself to the NASDAQ.

> **"Chief among the specialist obligations on the New York Stock Exchange is the requirement that trading in that stock will be fair and orderly at all times, and that it will have reasonable depth and continuity."**
>
> —THE SPECIALIST ASSOCIATION

The NYSE's Specialist System Versus the NASDAQ's Market-Maker System

To understand the origin of this volatility, we must look at the major structural differences between the New York Stock Exchange and the NASDAQ, and the way in which the bid-ask spread is maintained. In contrast to the NASDAQ, each New York Stock Exchange stock has one specialist who maintains an orderly market in that stock. The specialist risks his or her own capital to ensure that customers get fair executions, and that there is always liquidity in the marketplace.

> **"By risking their capital, Specialists help build a stairway of supply and demand to make price moves more orderly and less erratic."**
> —THE SPECIALIST ASSOCIATION

The specialist's job is to be the buyer and the seller of last resort, and to "smooth out" the buying and selling imbalances that occur throughout the trading day. This is done by being a buyer when the market needs buyers, and a seller when the market needs sellers. Thus the specialist has an extremely important job, because the burden to keep the market fair rests entirely upon his or her shoulders.

THE SPECIALIST AND THE TWO-SIDED MARKET

The specialist system on the New York Stock Exchange is the backbone that makes it by far the fairest and most orderly financial market in the world. The specialist will risk his or her own capital to ensure that customers get fair executions. He or she does this by quoting a two-sided market.

KM 10–10$\frac{1}{16}$ 5,000 × 5,000

In this example the specialist is a buyer of 5,000 shares of Kmart at 10 and a seller of 5,000 at 10$\frac{1}{16}$. The only reason the specialist is willing to risk trading capital to buy 5,000 shares at 10 in the first place is because he thinks he can turn right around and sell them at 10$\frac{1}{16}$ for a profit. That is his compensation for risking his trading capital to keep the markets orderly.

NASDAQ's Version of the Two-Sided Market

The main difference between the NYSE's specialist system and the NASDAQ's market-maker system is the way in which this two-sided market is maintained. While the NYSE has one specialist assigned to each stock, NASDAQ may have five or ten market makers who collectively share the burden of maintaining an orderly market.

NASDAQ's Two-Sided Market

On the NASDAQ the burden of maintaining an orderly market falls equally upon the group of market makers.

MICROSOFT (MSFT)

Market Maker Buys			Market Maker Sells		
10	GSCO	115	10	SLCK	$115\frac{1}{8}$
10	MSCO	115	10	MLCO	$115\frac{1}{8}$
10	MASH	115	10	BEST	$115\frac{1}{8}$
10	NITE	115	10	PRUS	$115\frac{1}{8}$
10	FBCO	115	10	RSSF	$115\frac{1}{8}$

As this example, Microsoft (MSFT), shows, there are five market makers bidding for stock, and five market makers offering stock for sale. Notice that among the five firms willing to buy 1,000 shares at 115 are Goldman Sachs (GSCO) and Morgan Stanley (MSCO). And notice also that among the five firms willing to sell 1,000 shares each at $115\frac{1}{8}$ are Merrill Lynch (MLCO) and Prudential (PRUS). This structure is profoundly different from that of the NYSE, where one and only one specialist makes the two-sided market.

Please do not be confused by the difference in how the NASDAQ and the NYSE reflect the number of shares on the bid and the ask. Sometimes it is abbreviated, sometimes it is not. On the NASDAQ, add 00 to the number. In other words, 10 means 1,000. On the NYSE, 1,000 will be reflected either as 10 or unabbreviated as 1,000, depending upon the quote service you use.

The Major Players on the NASDAQ

The day trader will come across the same Wall Street firms "making markets" in the vast universe of NASDAQ stocks. Among the most prominent are:

Goldman Sachs (GSCO)   Salomon Smith Barney (SBSH)
Morgan Stanley (MSCO)   Mayer Schweitzer (MASH)
Merrill Lynch (MLCO)   Herzog (HRZG)
Prudential (PRUS)   Lehman Brothers (LEHM)
First Boston (FBCO)   Hambrecht and Quist (HMQT)
Knight Securities (NITE)   Bear Stearns (BEST)

Why Do the Majority of Day Traders Gravitate Toward the NASDAQ?

The main reason for the NASDAQ market being the destination of choice among day traders is that, compared with the NYSE, the NASDAQ market is extremely inefficient, which is exactly what causes its volatility. In order to exploit the market for consistent profit, day traders use the NASDAQ to their advantage. To begin to understand why the NASDAQ market is so much more inefficient than the NYSE, we need to begin by examining NASDAQ Level II.

NASDAQ Level II

Without question, the one aspect of NASDAQ that day traders like most is the level of depth that the quoted market shows. A NASDAQ Level II quote screen lets the general public see something they are not allowed to see on the New York Stock Exchange: how "deep" the buyers and sellers go. In other words, if there are large buyers lurking "below" the market, or if there are large sellers sitting "above" the market, you will see them on the NASDAQ.

NASDAQ LEVEL II

The Level II screen is the main reason for many day traders gravitating toward NASDAQ stocks and away from NYSE stocks. This is of great benefit to day traders, particularly in volatile times, because it allows them to see potential buyers "lurking" below the market, and potential sellers "sitting" above the market.

Qualcomm (QCOM)

Market Maker Buys			Market Maker Sells		
10	GSCO	115	10	FBCO	$115\frac{3}{8}$
5	MLCO	115	10	HRZG	$115\frac{1}{2}$
4	MSCO	$114\frac{7}{8}$	30	ISLD	$115\frac{9}{16}$
20	MASH	$114\frac{3}{4}$	30	INCA	$115\frac{9}{16}$
2	NITE	$114\frac{5}{8}$	100	SLCK	$115\frac{5}{8}$

The depth of NASDAQ Level II alerts day traders to the fact that there is a sell imbalance outside the quoted market (SLCK is a seller of 10,000, up at $115\frac{5}{8}$). If this was a NYSE stock, you would have no way of knowing this.

One of the main reasons for day traders shying away from New York Stock Exchange listed stocks is because they do not like the fact that the specialist "conceals" the depth of the market. Only the specialist knows what is lurking below or above the market. As you know, this is not true on the NASDAQ. Let's look at another example.

Detecting Buyers and Sellers Outside the Market

For the purposes of illustration, let's assume that DoubleClick (DCLK) traded on both the NASDAQ and the New York Stock Exchange at the same time. In reality, this could never happen. But, for this example, imagine that it did. You pull up the quote, and here is how it looks:

DCLK   104–104¼   100 ×3,000
The inside quote says that 100 shares are willing to be bought at
104, and 3,000 shares are willing to be sold at 104¼.

On the New York Stock Exchange, the inside quote is all you are going to get. This quote shows a lopsided market: More stock willing to be sold at 104¼ than bought at 104. The conclusion: the stock is probably headed lower. But the inside quote doesn't tell the whole story. If we knew what was going on outside the quoted market, would that change our opinion of the stock?

For instance, what if there is a large institutional seller up at 104⅝₁₆? What if Goldman Sachs has a buy order for 9,000 shares $\frac{1}{16}$th point below the market, at 103¹⁵⁄₁₆? Would having this information be enough to change our minds about the stock? You bet it would. Furthermore, would there be any way of knowing this? Not on the New York Stock Exchange. The specialist knows, but he is certainly not going to give out any of that information to the investing public. The specialist is also fully aware of just how critical this information is in trying to predict if the next move in the stock is going to be higher or lower. Giving the information out to you and me severely limits the trading advantage that the specialist has over us. That is something he or she would never give up.

Fighting with One Hand Tied Behind Your Back

As you can see, for those who gravitate toward trading the most volatile stocks, if you can't see the depth of the market, it is like fighting the Wall Street trading firms with one hand tied behind your back. When you don't have the same supply and demand information on the stock that other traders have, what do you think your chances are of being on the right side of the trade?

Two Contradictory Pictures of Supply and Demand

In our imaginary example of a stock that trades on both the NYSE and the NASDAQ simultaneously, we see two contradictory perceptions of supply and demand.

NYSE: DCLK 104–104¼   100 × 3,000

While the specialist's quote shows a lopsided market to the downside, with more stock willing to be sold at 104 ¼ (3,000 shares) than bought at 104 (100 shares), NASDAQ Level II paints an entirely different picture of the supply and demand in the stock.

NASDAQ LEVEL II

DOUBLECLICK (DCLK)

1	MLCO	104	30	NITE	104¼
90	GSCO	$103^{15}/_{16}$	1	MASH	104⅜
90	MSCO	$103^{15}/_{16}$	1	SLCK	104½
90	FBCO	$103^{15}/_{16}$	1	RSSF	104⅝

The Level II screen shows strong buying support below the quoted market. Look at all of the firms willing to buy 9,000 shares at $103^{15}/_{16}$. And very little selling pressure above the market. Thus, on the NYSE, the stock appears to be headed lower. Yet on NASDAQ Level II, the stock clearly looks as if it is headed higher. This is why seeing the "depth" of the market is so critical when trading the most volatile stocks.

Isn't NASDAQ Fairer Than the NYSE?

At this point it is important that I make one thing clear. You may be getting the impression that the NASDAQ market is actually fairer and more orderly than the New York Stock Exchange. How can the latter possibly be considered a "fair" market if the specialist hides the "true" supply and demand in the stock from the investing public? Because the NASDAQ makes that information available to us, doesn't that make it fairer, and thus a better market in which to trade?

For reasons we will delve into later, it is essential to keep in the back of your mind that this is not the case. From the investing public's standpoint, and regardless of the fact that the NASDAQ does show "depth," the NYSE operates with a much higher degree of fairness, integrity, and efficiency. Perhaps if more people traded New York Stock Exchange stocks instead of NASDAQ stocks, the success rate among day traders would be greater than three out of ten. When you have finished this book, you will see why.

The very fact that so many day traders are able to make so much money trading NASDAQ stocks proves just how inefficient the market is. As we have said, you have three out of ten daytraders making a tremendous amount of money, and seven out of ten consistently losing it. So just because the NASDAQ market is inefficient and unfair, that doesn't mean that it can't be exploited for profit. But the day trader must understand just how inefficient the NASDAQ market is before he can trade on it success-fully.

The Wild West Shoot-Out

If the New York Stock Exchange is a fair and orderly market, the NASDAQ market is sometimes like a Wild West shoot-out. Day trading on these two markets is so fundamentally different that it is rare to see day traders who actively trade both markets simultaneously, and successfully. The very best in the business concentrate on one or the other, but not both. What does that tell you about the structure of these two markets, and how much they are at odds? Why do day traders have difficulty switching back and forth between the NASDAQ and the NYSE?

The Scalp Traders Versus the Momentum Trader

To answer this question, we have to examine the two major types of day traders: scalp traders and momentum traders. There are two fundamental differences between scalp traders and momentum traders: (1) the amount of stock they trade, and (2) the kinds of stocks they trade. Typically, scalp traders trade much larger blocks of stock than momentum traders, but they look for much smaller profits. A scalp trader may trade 2,000- or 4,000-share lots, and will typically look for only "razor-thin" profits of $\frac{1}{16}$ths, $\frac{1}{8}$ths, and $\frac{1}{4}$s. Because of the high level of risk involved in taking a 4,000-share position, scalp traders tend to gravitate toward stocks with much less

---

SCALP TRADERS TRADE "SIZE" BUT LOOK FOR RAZOR-THIN PROFITS

For instance, in the Rite Aid (RAD), the scalper would attempt to buy 4,000 at 7 and sell the stock at $7\frac{1}{16}$. If successful, the trader will have made a profit of $250.

RAD $7–7\frac{1}{16}$

In an ideal situation, the time it will take for the day trader to be in and out of this position may be only a few minutes or seconds. The scalp trader did not make $250 because the stock gapped higher or lower. Instead, the profit was made by exploiting the difference between the bid and the ask. In other words, by using limit orders, the scalp trader undercut the specialist by buying on the bid (7) and selling on the ask ($7\frac{1}{16}$). The $250 profit that the scalp trader made is $250 less profit that the specialist will make that day.

RAD $7–7\frac{1}{16}$

Notice how the day trader made this $\frac{1}{16}$th profit: not by trading against the specialist, but instead by "mirroring" his moves and trading with him. The specialist was a buyer at 7 and a seller at $7\frac{1}{16}$, and so was the day trader. By undercutting the specialist's ability to "capture" the spread, the day trader is able to step in front, and essentially "steal" the profit from him.

---

volatility than those that the momentum trader may trade. That is why the scalp trader's domain is the New York Stock Exchange. The NASDAQ is simply too volatile for this kind of trading strategy.

The Momentum Trader

Unlike the scalp trader, the momentum trader attempts to profit from volatility as much as he attempts to profit from the spread. Instead of making $\frac{1}{16}$ths and $\frac{1}{8}$ths, the momentum trader looks for larger profits: $\frac{1}{4}$s, $\frac{1}{2}$s, or higher. The momentum trader's domain is NASDAQ stocks, because the stocks capable of producing a $\frac{1}{2}$ or full-point movement in only a few seconds or minutes are typically the most volatile NASDAQ stocks. For the risk involved, the momentum trader usually won't trade the kind of large "size" that a scalp trader trades on the NYSE.

Interpreting the Bid Size and the Ask Size Is the Scalp Trader's Key to Profit

As we touched upon earlier, the day trader who trades New York Stock Exchange stocks does not have the luxury of seeing the "depth" of the market. Unlike NASDAQ Level II, on the NYSE only the specialist knows the "true" supply and demand that lurks outside the parameters of the quoted market for the stock. In our example above, the scalp trader is making a big "leap of faith" when he buys 4,000 shares at 7. There are many things he doesn't know. Is there a large institutional buy order below the market at $6^{15}\!/_{16}$? Is there a large sell order sitting above the market at $7\frac{1}{8}$? The only one who knows the answer to these questions is the specialist.

The point here is that when taking that kind of risk, the scalp trader cannot afford to "fly blind." How can you leave anything to chance when taking a 4,000-share position? For this reason, scalp traders look to another "source" for guidance before making any buy or sell decision. That "source" is the bid size and the ask size.

The Bid and the Ask Do Not Tell the Whole Story

It is not enough for the scalp trader to rely upon the bid and the ask when making a trading decision. Because the "depth" of the market is concealed by the specialist, the only true measure of supply and demand on the NYSE that the scalper can go on is reflected in the bid size and the ask size. The bid size is the number of shares willing to be bought at the bid price, and the ask size is the number of shares willing to be sold at the ask price.

The only "inside" clue that the specialist will give the scalp trader about the future direction of the stock is the bid size and the ask size. Remember the basic rules of supply and demand: When there is more stock willing to be bought than sold, the stock is probably headed higher. And when there is more stock willing to be sold than bought, the tendency is for the stock to trade down.

A DEMAND IMBALANCE INDICATES THAT SILICON GRAPHICS IS HEADED HIGHER . . .

20,000 shares are willing to be bought at 13; 2,000 shares willing to be sold at $13\frac{1}{16}$.

SGI	13–$13\frac{1}{16}$	$20{,}000 \times 2{,}000$

The bid and the ask in this example provide no guidance, but the bid size and the ask size provide a clear indication that the stock is headed higher! This is a classic example of a demand imbalance: There is more stock willing to be bought at 13 than there is willing to be sold at $13\frac{1}{16}$.

. . . but seconds later, a supply imbalance indicates that the next move is lower . . .

SGI	13–$13\frac{1}{16}$	$500 \times 10{,}000$

Unlike seconds earlier, there is now more stock willing to be sold at $13\frac{1}{16}$ than bought at 13. 10,000 shares are willing to be sold, but only 500 shares are willing to be bought. A lopsided market. More sellers than buyers. Stock is probably headed lower.

The day trader can learn a great deal from studying the bid size and the ask size. It is not 100 percent foolproof, but over time it is a very accurate short-term indicator of where a stock is headed. It is important to emphasize that this is a *short-term* indicator. Bid size and ask size will predict where the stock is headed in the next few seconds, or minutes, but it will not help you with longer-term trends. If you tried to use the bid size and the ask size to predict where a stock will be trading four hours from now, it wouldn't help you. But the beauty of this is that the scalp trader doesn't care what the stock will do in four hours. He wants and needs to know where it is headed *right now.*

READING LOPSIDED MARKETS

The bid size and the ask size are a NYSE stock's single most valuable predictor of future price movement because they reflect supply and demand imbalances.

RAD $7–7\frac{1}{16}$ 20,000 × 100

paints a much different picture from

RAD $7–7\frac{1}{16}$ 100 × 20,000

Lopsided stocks are those with more stock willing to be bought than sold, or more stock willing to be sold than bought. Lopsided markets do not stay lopsided forever. The stock price will quickly adjust to correct the imbalance. The stock will move lower if it needs to find buyers, and higher if it needs to find sellers.

A supply imbalance	*A demand imbalance*
100 × 20,000	20,000 × 100
probably headed lower	*probably headed higher*

Why Do Scalp Traders Gravitate Toward the New York Stock Exchange?

The question may arise as to why scalp traders gravitate toward the New York Stock Exchange instead of NASDAQ. Wouldn't it be easier to be profitable on NASDAQ, where you can look at a Level II screen to detect supply and demand imbalances, and therefore not have to rely upon the NYSE's bid size and ask size? The answer is no. The reason for this being the case sheds some light on just how unfair the NASDAQ market is.

The scalp trader is able to make a living only because he exploits a loophole in the rules that govern the trading of NYSE stocks. The loophole is that the specialist is required to give priority to a customer order over his own order. This allows the scalp trader to buy and sell at the same exact prices as the specialist. The NASDAQ does not honor the same "fair" order-handling rules. Because of this the scalp trader is prevented from making a successful living if he uses this strategy on NASDAQ stocks. We will revisit this issue in detail in later chapters. For now, keep in the back of your mind that the structure and the rules of the NASDAQ make it all but impossible for this kind of trading strategy to be profitable.

Momentum Traders Look to Market-Maker Activity, Not Bid Size and Ask Size

Unlike the scalp trader on the New York Stock Exchange, the NASDAQ momentum trader does not rely upon bid size or ask size. In stark contrast with the New York Stock Exchange, which has one centralized "floor," with the majority of the order flow going through it, the NASDAQ market is "all over the place." You have buyers and sellers simultaneously exchanging stock on different "channels" completely apart from each other. Goldman Sachs might be selling to Morgan Stanley at the same exact time that Merrill Lynch is buying from First Boston. With all these cross-currents of activity, bid size and ask size are not going to accurately reflect the real supply and demand situation in the stock.

So what do momentum traders look for? Just like scalp traders, momentum traders look for temporary supply and demand imbalances. But they find these not by reading the changes in bid size and ask size, but by interpreting the movements of the market makers themselves.

A WALL OF BUYERS WILL POWER THE STOCK HIGHER

On the NASDAQ when a wall of buyers appears on the bid at the same price, it is usually an indication that buying pressure has come into the market.

RED HAT (RHAT)

Market Maker Buys			Market Maker Sells		
10	GSCO	101	3	PRUS	$101\frac{1}{4}$
10	MLCO	101	2	ISLD	$101\frac{5}{16}$
20	MSCO	101	3	REDI	$101\frac{3}{8}$
10	ATTN	101	1	MASH	$101\frac{7}{16}$

In the above example, the market makers are "bunched" at 101 and the bids are building up. Stocks move in the path of least resistance, so the chances are that this stock is headed higher, not lower.

Therefore, the momentum trader's primary job is to interpret the subtle movements of the buyers and the sellers on NASDAQ Level II. Let's look at another example, but this time in a stock that looks like it is headed lower.

Thin Stocks Versus Thick Stocks

You may be surprised to know that as much as there is a fundamental difference between scalp trading on the NYSE and trading on the NASDAQ, there is just as much of a contrast within segments in the NASDAQ universe. There is a huge difference in the approach and mechanics of trading a bellweather stock like Microsoft (MSFT) and trading a highflier like JDS Uniphase (JDSU). That is what we will examine now.

One of the big misperceptions about the NASDAQ is that the "darlings" of the investing public are also the "darlings" of the day traders. This is not true. You may be surprised to know that "blue chip" NASDAQ stocks like Microsoft, Dell, Oracle, and Intel are not the first choice of the day trading community. These widely held stocks are simply too competitive and efficient for most day traders to make money by trading them. In other words, there are other areas of the NASDAQ market in which it is much easier to trade.

So what is it about the composition of these bellweather stocks that day traders do not like? What makes them so efficient, and thus so difficult for day traders to trade? It is something that we call "thickness."

CISCO IS A "THICK" STOCK

Cisco is considered a "thick" stock because there are many buyers and sellers at each given price level. This means that it takes massive buying pressure to move the stock higher by even $\frac{1}{2}$ a point.

Cisco (CSCO)

Market Maker Buys			Market Maker Sells		
5	CSCO	110	10	GSCO	$110\frac{1}{8}$
3	BEST	110	10	MLCO	$110\frac{1}{8}$
10	NEED	110	10	MSCO	$110\frac{1}{8}$
9	PRUS	110	10	REDI	$110\frac{1}{8}$
10	FBCO	110	10	SELZ	$110\frac{1}{8}$
10	ISLD	110	5	CIBC	$110\frac{1}{8}$
20	ARCA	$109\frac{15}{16}$	14	ADAM	$110\frac{3}{16}$
11	SHWD	$109\frac{7}{8}$	15	MONT	$110\frac{3}{16}$

Also, the stock is so liquid that the bid-ask spreads are extremely narrow, helping the investing public but hurting day traders, who look for the juicy profits that wide spreads provide. Day traders look for more action in other stocks.

As the example of Cisco shows, there are simply too many buyers and sellers in the same price range to get any meaningful movement out of the stock in a short period of time. The more players involved, the narrower the spread, and thus the more competitive the stock. Day traders do not want this kind of competition because it severely limits the profit potential that may exist.

This sheds light on one of the major themes of day trading. The more active the stock, the more efficient the stock. The more efficient the stock, the harder it is for the day trader to make a profit. That is why "thick" stocks like Dell, Intel, and Microsoft are shunned by the majority of day traders. While momentum traders gravitate away from "thick" stocks like

Cisco, Oracle, and Sun Microsystems, they lean toward "thin" stocks like Juniper, Rambus, Exodus, and DoubleClik. They like "thin" stocks for the same reason that they despise "thick" stocks.

RAMBUS IS A THIN STOCK

Rambus (RMBS) is considered a thin stock. Unlike Cisco, the bid-ask spread is sometimes larger than 1 point. In addition, there is a very small amount of stock for sale at each price level.

RAMBUS (RMBS)

Market Maker Buys			Market Maker Sells		
1	PRUS	285	1	GSCO	286
1	NEED	$284\frac{1}{2}$	1	MSCO	$286\frac{1}{2}$
1	SLCK	284	1	MLCO	287
1	ISLD	$283\frac{1}{2}$	1	FBCO	$287\frac{1}{2}$

As a consequence, it takes only a very small amount of buying pressure to send the stock up higher by several points. In fact, one buyer of 400 shares would send the stock from 286 to $287\frac{1}{2}$ in about two seconds. With Cisco, it would probably take thousands of buy orders to get the same $1\frac{1}{2}$-point move.

The Elephant Through the Front Door

As you can see, a measly 400-share buy order would drive the "thin" stock up $1\frac{1}{2}$ points in a matter of seconds! Did you ever wonder why a stock like Rambus has 20- and 30-point intra-day swings, but Dell and Intel never do? When a thin stock is bombarded with buy orders, it is like trying to fit an elephant through your front door. A lucky few are able to get their hands on cheap stock, but the majority of potential buyers are simply unable to accumulate stock at "reasonable" price levels. In fact, there may be such a small amount of stock for sale at each price level that it will completely distort the normal parameters of supply and demand. In other words, there may be no limit to how far a buyer may have to chase the stock before he gets his hands on it. This is why a thin stock like RMBS has gone up 60 points in a a single trading day. Day traders love a situation like this: They take advantage of both the wide bid-ask spread and the insane volatility.

The hallmark of a "thin" stock is that it takes only the slightest buying pressure to send the stock soaring higher, and very little selling pressure to drive it into the ground. Thin stocks are characterized by a combination of wide bid-ask spreads, a tiny amount of stock for sale at all times, and only a handful of market makers. The thinner the stock, the fewer market participants involved. The fewer market participants, the more inefficient the stock. The more inefficient the stock, the easier it is for the day trader to exploit it for profit.

It is very important for the day trader to have a firm grasp of the mechanics behind the price movement of a thin stock versus that of a thick stock. In other words, how can a 400-share buy order drive a thin stock like Rambus or Juniper up several points in only a few seconds, while that same 400-share buy order wouldn't even cause Microsoft, Oracle, or Apple to budge $\frac{1}{16}$th of a point?

It is simply a matter of supply and demand. All financial markets are organized around the basic premise that the cheapest stock for sale in the marketplace always gets sold first. When all of the cheap stock is grabbed, buyers have to pay higher prices to get stock. The thick stocks always have plenty of stock for sale; the thin stocks don't.

The Ferrari Dealership Versus the Ford Dealership

To draw an analogy, compare a Ferrari dealership to that of your local Ford dealership. There are always plenty of Fords for sale, but Ferraris are few and far between. The Ford dealership may have three hundred cars sitting on the lot, but the Ferrari dealership may have only two or three. What if there are only three Ferraris in the showroom, but ten people that day demand them? What if five of those people want to drive home a Ferrari so badly that they say they will pay any price to get it? What happens to the price of Ferraris? You may have a $150,000 Ferrari sell that day for $200,000 or more. Yet if those same five people wanted to buy Fords, it would not affect the price at all. There are enough Fords on the lot to absorb the buying pressure. That is exactly the difference between a thin stock and a thick stock. The blue chip stocks like Microsoft, Cisco, and Dell are the Ford dealerships, and the high-fliers like Rambus, Juniper, and Exodus are the Ferrari dealerships.

Let's look at another example of how this phenomenon plays out. This time, we will compare the effect of a 500-share buy order on the price of Juniper versus that of Microsoft.

BUYING STOCK ONE PRICE LEVEL AT A TIME

Juniper Networks (JNPR)

Market Maker Buys			Market Maker Sells		
1	PRUS	202	1	NEED	203
1	SLCK	$201\frac{1}{2}$	1	GSCO	$203\frac{1}{2}$
1	FBCO	201	1	NITE	204
1	MASH	$200\frac{1}{2}$	1	MLCO	$204\frac{1}{2}$
1	RSSF	200	1	MSCO	205

A 500-share buy order in JNPR will send the stock from 203 to 205 in seconds.

1st step: 100 shares bought from NEED at 203, with 400 remaining to buy

2nd step: 100 shares bought from GSCO at $203\frac{1}{2}$, with 300 remaining to buy

3rd step: 100 shares bought from NITE at 204, with 200 remaining to buy

4th step: 100 shares bought from MLCO at $204\frac{1}{2}$ with 100 remaining to buy

5th step: 100 shares bought from MSCO at 205, to complete the order

Because the stock was so thin, the 500 shares were bought one price level at a time, 100 shares at 203, another 100 at $203\frac{1}{2}$, 100 more at 204, $204\frac{1}{2}$, and, finally, 205. Each 100-share lot "ticked" the stock higher by $\frac{1}{2}$ point.

Now if we use this same 500-share example, but replace a "thin" stock like Juniper with a "thick" one like Microsoft, we have an entirely different outcome.

The Pendulum Swings Both Ways in Thin Stocks

The danger of trading thin stocks is that the same phenomenon that sends them rocketing higher can also drive them right into the ground. The slightest sell-off hurts these stocks more than any others in the entire marketplace. If everyone heads for the exits at the same time, you have the same effect as when they all piled in, but in reverse. *The elephant that got stuck on the way in the door also gets stuck on the way out.*

No Exit

Thin stocks are the last place you want to be during panic selling. They do not have enough "mass" to absorb the selling pressure.

Phone.com (PHCM)

Market Maker Buys				Market Maker Sells		
1	GSCO	116		1	GRUN	117
2	MLCO	115⅝		1	OLDE	117⅝
1	NITE	115		1	COWN	118⅛
3	MASH	114		1	DLJP	119

It would take only a 600-share sell order to drive PHCM down 2 full points, from 116 to 114. Here's how the stock would drop 2 points:

1st phase: 100 shares sold to GSCO at 116, leaving 500 remaining

2nd phase: 200 shares sold to MLCO at 115⅝, leaving 300 remaining

3rd phase: 100 shares sold to NITE at 115, leaving 200 remaining

4th phase: 200 shares sold to MASH at 114, completing the sell order

Imagine what would happen if you needed to sell 2,000 shares of a thin stock during a market sell-off. You would have a big problem on your hands because there are no buyers anywhere. Even worse, imagine what a 10,000-share sell order would do to a thin stock. Theoretically, it could drive it down 5 points or more. A thick stock like Microsoft or Dell, on the other hand, wouldn't even feel a 10,000-share sell order because it has the mass to absorb it.

Selling at the Wrong Time Makes You Your Own Worst Enemy

"Sell when you can, not when you have to." That is the conventional wisdom among successful day traders. There is no better evidence of why you must do this than the last example. In a thin stock you do not have the luxury of waiting until the stock starts dropping to sell it. If you do, you won't be able to get out at a reasonable price. This drives home the fact that you have to buy on weakness and sell on strength, particularly if you trade large amounts ("size"). Otherwise, if you wait until the stock runs out of steam before dumping it, you will pound the stock right into the ground. To add fuel to the fire, you need only one or two other sellers doing the same exact thing to have the stock spiral out of control.

Thin Stocks Fall Very Easily Out of Favor

The irony of trading "thin" stocks is that they don't stay "thin" forever. If you went back in time, you would see that the technology bellweathers like Microsoft, Intel, Dell, and Cisco' traded five years ago like Rambus, Juniper, and Ariba trade today. Today's blue chips were yesterday's "thin" highfliers. This is why it is so important to never get married to a single stock. The makeup and composition of every stock will change over time. What makes the stock a good one today may not make it good to trade in a week, a month, or a year from now. Among day traders, today's favorable stock could become tomorrow's unfavorable one. In other words, as evidenced by stocks like Dell and Intel, today's "thin" stock could become tomorrow's "thick" one.

Perhaps the best examples of this in today's market are stocks like Yahoo!, Amazon.com, and eBay. These were once the "darlings" of day traders back in 1998 and early 1999. But from the day trader's perspective, all three of these stocks have become much more difficult to trade now than they were back then. Many of the day traders who once made money on them don't even trade them anymore.

So What Makes a Stock Go from Being In Favor Among Day Traders to Out of Favor?

Why did stocks like Yahoo!, Amazon.com, and eBay go from being the darlings of many day traders one year to being avoided by them the next? *It is because their composition changed from being "thin" stocks to being "thick" ones!* Here's the problem. Naturally, day traders will gravitate toward those stocks that they feel have the best chance of being profitable. In the beginning the combination of wide bid-ask spreads and a limited number of market players create the kind of environment where "easy money" is made. This is, of course, before they are "discovered" by the rest of the investing world, including other day traders.

The easier the money, the more day traders become involved. It becomes a self-fulfilling prophecy. Opportunities for easy money do not last forever. Eventually so many day traders get involved in the stock that it no longer becomes "easy" to trade. The "juice" that made these stocks so attractive in the first place gets squeezed out when too many traders enter the scene. Wide bid-ask spreads become narrow, and the competition to capitalize on the movements becomes too intense.

Nothing Ruins a Stock Quicker Than a Stock Split

Another irony among day traders is that the more a stock splits, the harder it becomes to trade it profitably. This flies in the face of the conventional wisdom of the investing public, who think that stock splits are the best thing since sliced bread. The problem for day traders is that once it splits, the stock gets a larger "float." A stock with a bigger "float" becomes a thicker stock. When the stock has only 10 million shares outstanding, the market is thin. But after the stock rockets higher and the company splits it 3 for 1, you now have three times as much stock outstanding. If it took only 2,000 shares of buying to drive the stock higher by 1 point before, after it splits it may take 6,000 shares to get the same move. Why? *The bigger the "float," the more sellers per price level.* Thus it can be said that the real reason for stocks like Microsoft, Intel, and Dell, no longer being good to trade is because they have split so many times.

Once today's "darlings," like DoubleClik and Exodus, split several more times, they will no longer be considered "darlings." Even a stock like Ameritrade (AMTD), which split in mid-1999, was a wonderful stock to trade before the split. Now it is terrible. In fact, it could very well be that by the time you read this book, stocks like Rambus and Juniper will no longer be as "thin" as I have described them here. Rest assured that, if they are no longer "thin," there will be plenty of other stocks to take their place. (For the latest and most up-to-date list of thin stocks "in favor" among day traders, as well as those that have become "thick," or out of favor, visit my website at *www.farrelltrading.com.*)

So Why Is the Market-Maker System So Much More Volatile Than the Specialist System?

Thus far we have explained the major differences between scalp trading on the New York Stock Exchange and momentum trading on the NASDAQ. We then examined the fundamental differences between "thin" stocks and "thick" stocks within the NASDAQ universe, and delved into the mechanics behind a stock like Juniper moving 40 points in a day but Microsoft never doing this. But we still haven't answered the main question: Why is the market-maker system itself so much more volatile than the specialist system?

The Art of Paying Through the Market

Perhaps the single biggest contrast between the specialist system on the NYSE and the market-makers system is the issue of "paying through" the market. On NASDAQ day traders and market makers alike are allowed to buy and sell stock outside the quoted market. Let's look at an example.

Paying Through Completely Distorts Supply and Demand

In the most volatile market conditions, "paying through" completely distorts the normal parameters of supply and demand. In our above example, imagine that you had two day traders who were in a panic situation: One thought the stock was headed higher, the other thought it was headed lower. Simultaneously, in the confusion one pays through the market to buy stock while the other pays through the market to sell stock. The result? You would see the stock "print" at $214\frac{3}{4}$, and then immediately at 218! NEED would be buying stock at $214\frac{3}{4}$ at the same time that NITE was selling it at 218!

To take it a step farther, imagine ten or twenty day traders doing that all at once. If you were sitting at home watching your quote screen, and didn't understand the concept of paying through, it would leave you dumbfounded as to what was going on in the stock. You would see the stock recklessly trading all over the map: 214¾ ... 218 ... 215 ... 217¾ ... 214⅞. And you must remember that in volatile times, all of this movement could happen in a span of only one or two seconds.

Why Isn't Paying Through Done on the New York Stock Exchange?

Remember, unlike the NASDAQ, the specialist system conceals the depth of the market. If we can't see who the additional buyers are *below* the market, and who the additional sellers are *above* the market, how can we possibly "pay through" to trade stock with them? This is also one of the main reasons for the New York Stock Exchange being considered a fairer and more orderly market than the NASDAQ. How can a market be considered orderly when you have stock trading all over the map, at 214¾ at precisely the same time that it is trading at 218? This is exactly the problem. As we have said, when the volatility gets out of control, it is the investing public at the biggest disadvantage. Hopefully, this sheds some light on why the NASDAQ market is so much more volatile and inefficient than the New York Stock Exchange. A "thin" NASDAQ stock in which day traders are paying $2 through the market to buy stock is much more likely to move 40 points in a day than a stock that is trading under the close supervision of a specialist.

2

Gouging the Customer: Dirty Little Secrets of the Online Brokerage Firms

Did you ever wonder why it is next to impossible to use a regular online broker to actively day trade the most volatile NASDAQ stocks profitably, yet you can rely upon those same online brokers to trade New York Stock Exchange stocks profitably? Why is it that the online brokers are more apt to give you a better execution on the NYSE than they do on the NASDAQ? Why do the most successful momentum traders refuse to use regular online brokers to execute their trades? This chapter will answer those questions.

A False Sense of Security

All of the advances in trading technology have created a false sense of security among novice online traders. In the beginning many fail to see just how much of a disadvantage they are at when they use a regular online broker to execute their trades, particularly in the most volatile NASDAQ stocks. As day traders, *we are not on a level playing field*. To think we are is a very dangerous thing, because many of us will learn the hard way just how uneven this playing field really is.

The first thing that we must do is understand the distinction between regular online brokers and higher-cost, direct-access trading systems. From the day trader's perspective, the difference between the two is like night and day. When we refer to the term "online brokers," we mean the mainstream, deep-discount companies you see on television every single day. These are the ones that offer trade commissions of $10, $8, and some even cheaper than that. The popularity of online trading has made many of these online brokers, such as Ameritrade, E-Trade, Waterhouse, Datek, Brown, and Sure-trade, to name a few, household names.

These online brokers are very different in nature from the higher-end, direct-access trading systems that professional traders use. In direct-access trading, you are not paying a sub-$10 trade commission. Instead, you are paying a slightly higher price. Why do these direct-access systems cost more? As we will learn in this chapter, they cost more simply because *no one is trying to profit at your expense.* (Check my website at *www.farrelltrading.com* for an up-to-date list of the best and worst direct-access trading systems and online brokers.)

Direct-Access Trading Eliminates the Middleman

Why is the execution so much faster with direct access? Because your order is being carried into the marketplace directly by you, the day trader. In other words, the middleman is eliminated. This is another way of saying that *the online brokers are in the business of trading against their customers, while direct-access trading firms are not!* In a nutshell, this means that you cannot use a regular online broker to trade the most volatile stocks because you will get horrible executions.

The poor executions may not make much of a difference if you are someone who trades only a few times a week, but for the rest of us who may make fifty trades in a single day, these bad executions alone can be the difference between making a living and losing money. The root of the problem lies in the fact that many times the online brokers do not have your best interests in mind.

The Online Brokers Are in the Business of Trading Against Their Customers

So if getting you the best execution is not always the online broker's top priority, what is? *It is making ¹⁄₁₆th, ¹⁄₈th, or ¹⁄₄ point on your trade!* That is the sole reason for many of these firms being in business. In other words, they are in the business of capturing the spread. As you will learn in this chapter, the cheap cost of the trade commissions that the online brokers offer is nothing more than a gimmick. If you need evidence of this, look at those online brokers who now offer free trades to some customers. Free trades! *They do not make their money on the trade commission, they make it by taking the other side of your trade.*

Unfortunately, as much as technological advances have altered the landscape of Wall Street, some things never change. Wall Street, as you know, has always been in the business of trading against its customers, and in the world of online trading, it is no different. As I said earlier, look at the cheap cost of the online trade in the same way that you look at the free "comps" at a Las Vegas casino: It is a way to lure customers in the door. In other words, these online brokers are willing to pay a small price to get your business because they think that down the line they can ultimately make money on you.

An Inherent Conflict of Interest

The problem with the online brokers is that they have an inherent conflict of interest. By entering a trade online, you are entrusting your hard-earned money to someone who is in a position to profit at your expense. But remember, this is the time-honored tradition on Wall Street—any profit a brokerage firm makes is made at the expense of the investing public.

Remember that we have said over and over, if you pay the spread on every trade, it will be impossible to make a living as a day trader. Now think about this: When you use an online broker, the online broker is also trying to make the spread. But guess what? *The online broker is trying to make the spread on you, at your expense!* That is why, from the day trader's perspective, using an online broker to trade the most volatile stocks is a complete absurdity. If as a day trader your main function is to "make the spread," why would you ever put yourself in the position of handing your order to someone who is trying to do the same thing in the market that you are, except at your expense? How can you possibly buy and sell stocks for a living when the firm executing your buys and sells is, in the process, trying to exploit you?

Market Orders Are the Way Online Brokers Make Their Money

We also said earlier that the single easiest way to lose money as a day trader is to use market orders. The analogy we used was to the sucking sound of a vacuum cleaner, in which your money was being sucked right out of your wallet. This fact is magnified when you use an online broker.

THE ONLINE BROKER HAS A LICENSE TO STEAL YOUR MONEY ON MARKET ORDERS

By using a market order, you are giving the online broker a license to steal your money! Why is that? Because you are allowing them the right to take the other side of your trade. Imagine, in this example, that you place a buy order of 1,000 shares of Exodus (EXDS) when the spread is ¼ point wide, at 100 to 100¼.

EXDS   100–100¼

Basically, the online broker will sell the stock to you at 100¼, then go into the market and buy it for himself at 100. You thought you got a great deal because you paid only $8 for the trade, but what you didn't realize was, by using a market order, you left $250 on the table. In other words, you allowed the online broker to make $250 at your expense! That is why the trades are so cheap.

First Dirty Little Secret: Payment for Order Flow

One of the ways in which the online brokers have tried to steer clear of the inherent conflict of interest they face is by something called "payment for order flow." "Payment for order flow" is one of the darkest and most controversial secrets in the world of online trading. Essentially, the online brokerage firms that use "payment for order flow" don't attempt to trade against their customers directly. Instead, and even worse, *they sell the order to someone else who does.*

Think about this for a moment: *Someone is literally paying money for the right to take the other side of your trade!* Do you think they are paying for that right because they think they are going to lose money? Do they pay money for the right to execute your order because they are your "friend," and they are genuinely interested in getting you the best possible price? Of course not! They are "buying" the orders because they feel reasonably certain that they can use their trading edge to exploit you for their own profit.

> "The Commission has long stressed to firms the importance of obtaining the best possible price when they route their customers' orders. They simply can't let payment for order flow or other relationships or inducements determine where they do business. That's why I have directed our examiners to focus in on firms' order routing practices in an examination sweep. I urge all firms to review their practices to ensure they're doing right by their customers."
>
> —ARTHUR LEVITT, CHAIRMAN
> *Securities and Exchange Commission,* The New York Times, *May 4, 1999*

For the market makers who engage in the business of paying for order flow, where are the profits coming from, and at whose expense are they made? *They are made at your expense.* When you are a buyer, the market maker will gladly sell to you. And when you are a seller, the market makers are drooling, wanting to buy the stock back from you. To gain a better understanding of why trading firms will actually go to great lengths to buy your order, let's look at a real-life experiment I did in March 2000 involving Raytheon (RTN.B), a New York Stock Exchange–listed stock. The whole basis of my experiment was to see what would happen if I used a market order. Here's how the market looked:

RTN.B   19–19⅛   **5,300 × 2,000**

I entered a buy order for 2,000 shares at "market" and got an immediate execution at 19⅛. This was a fair execution because that was the price at which stock was for sale.

The Order Was Routed Away from the Floor of the New York Stock Exchange

However, when I went back and examined the "prints," I noticed something very strange. This was a New York Stock Exchange stock, yet the trade was not executed on the floor of the NYSE. It had been routed to a regional exchange! But that was not 100 percent of the story. The peculiar thing about this was, whoever filled my order at 19⅛ immediately bought the stock for themselves at 19¹⁄₁₆! In other words, the market maker made ¹⁄₁₆th, or $125, at my expense. Why was my order filled at 19⅛? If it was that easy to buy stock at 19¹⁄₁₆, shouldn't I, as the customer, have received the benefit of the better "fill" at 19¹⁄₁₆? Don't the online brokers have a responsibility to their customers to give them the best possible execution?

Second Dirty Little Secret: Routing Your Order Away from the Exchange

> "All firms—whether on-line, discount or full service—have an obligation to ensure the best execution of their customers' orders. That is not just good business practice, it's a legal obligation. Firms have this same duty to their customers to find the best prices—whether they charge $10 per trade or $100 per trade."
>
> —ARTHUR LEVITT, CHAIRMAN,
> *Securities and Exchange Commission,* The New York Times, *May 4, 1999*

The Online Brokers Undercut the Specialist's Ability to Make the Spread

You may be wondering why the online broker routed my order away from the floor of the New York Stock Exchange. The answer is very simple: If the market order had been sent down to the floor, *the specialist would be the one making the spread!* By sending it to another exchange, the online broker is able to undercut the specialist and reap the benefits of making the spread for himself. This kind of thing goes on all the time, and at some point it must come to an end.

> "Customers save hundreds of millions of dollars each year when their orders are executed at the Specialist's post."
>
> —THE SPECIALIST ASSOCIATION

The fact of the matter is, when an order is routed away from the floor of the NYSE, the customer is the one who loses out. Nine out of ten times, you will get a better execution on the floor of the NYSE, under the supervision of the specialist, than you would when your order is unscrupulously routed to one of the smaller, less active, regional exchanges. This is one of the ways in which the online brokers put their own best interests ahead of their customers.

Third Dirty Little Secret: Mishandling of Customer Orders

> "In far too many cases, limit orders are being mishandled by market intermediaries and not being exposed to the market as required."
>
> —ARTHUR LEVITT, CHAIRMAN,
> *Securities and Exchange Commission,* The New York Times, *March, 17, 2000*

Going Undercover to Prove How Rampant the Mishandling of Customer Orders Is

If you are under the impression that online brokers do not mishandle customer orders, you are wrong. I did an "undercover" experiment on March 12, 2000, that proves just how rampant the problem of mishandling customer orders is, particularly on the NASDAQ. In this experiment I used two different low-volatility stocks: MCI preferred (symbol MCICP on the NASDAQ) and ConEdison "Quics" (symbol EDL on the NYSE). In both examples, the spread was at least ⅛th point wide. And, in both examples, I entered a limit order to buy 100 shares between the bid and the ask prices.

The goal here was to see if my online broker would reflect my limit order in the marketplace, as is required by the rules. You would think that in this day and age both the NYSE buy order and the NASDAQ buy order would be handled by my online broker with the same degree of integrity and fairness. This could not be farther from the truth.

It is not surprising that the online broker reflected my NYSE order in the marketplace. One of the benefits of trading NYSE stocks is that, to a certain extent, the online brokers are required to honor the specialist's fair-market rules. Don't be fooled into thinking that these rules will always protect you from getting bad executions—they won't. It is just that when trading NYSE stocks, and using limit orders, you are steering clear of many of the "shady" practices that cost other day traders money. However, as our experiment shows, below, this is unfortunately not true on the NASDAQ.

| 2 | OLDE | 22⅜ | 10 | PRUS | 22¾ |
| 20 | PRUS | 22⁵⁄₁₆ | 1 | FBRC | 22¾ |

At 12:42 I entered a buy order for 100 shares of MCICP at 22⁹⁄₁₆. Several minutes went by and the market did not change! Where was my buy order? In a galaxy far, far away? It was nowhere to be found. This is proof that my online broker had mishandled my order. I wanted to buy stock at 22⁹⁄₁₆, and my online broker, if he had my best interests in mind, would have carried my order into the marketplace and reflected the 22⁹⁄₁₆ bid. As you can see, this is not what he did.

If you ever want to have some fun with this kind of thing, try the experiment for yourself. And then after several minutes go by and the NASDAQ buy order is not reflected, call up your online broker and ask why. Do you know what he or she will say? *The order is being "worked."* On whose behalf is this order being worked? Certainly not mine.

When I was a trader at Gruntal, the concept of "working an order" meant that you shopped the order around to different houses on Wall Street. In other words, you called brokerage firms like Goldman Sachs, Merrill Lynch, and DLJ and asked them if they had any interest in selling your stock. Usually, the only orders that got "worked" were those of large institutions: share orders of 20,000 or 50,000. In our example with MCICP, to think that some market maker who works on behalf of the online broker is diligently shopping my measly 100-share order around Wall Street to get it executed is laughable. All they would have to do to help me out is reflect the order in the marketplace, where everyone can see it, instead of holding it and trying to trade against me.

Why was my NYSE buy order reflected in the market, but my NASDAQ order wasn't? We can conclude that the NASDAQ is far behind the NYSE in fairness. There is a larger "gray area" in the rules regarding the handling of customer orders on the NASDAQ, which puts the investing public at a severe disadvantage. This "gray area" is exactly what gives the online brokers the leeway to mishandle limit orders in an attempt to profit at the investor's expense. Remember that Wall Street will always try to get away with everything it can, and this is yet another example of that. If you ever wondered why the best momentum traders on Wall Street refuse to trade NASDAQ stocks using regular online brokers, this is why.

This Is Exactly What Led to the Creation of ECNs

What happened to me in this example has been happening on the NASDAQ for many years. In fact, day traders got so frustrated with the idea that their orders were being intentionally mishandled by the market makers on the NASDAQ that, basically, they created their own private trading networks. These day traders got together and said, "If the market makers refuse to reflect our orders in the marketplace, we will create our own private trading networks that will." These are what are now called ECNs, or electronic communications networks, like Island (ISLD), Attain (ATTN), Instinet (INCA), and Archipelago (ARCA).

ECNs GIVE THE DAY TRADER WHAT THE ONLINE BROKERS CANNOT—EQUAL FOOTING

If I had used an ECN like Island (ISLD) instead of an online broker, my bid at 22⁹/₁₆ would have immediately been reflected in the marketplace. Notice that my bid through (ISLD) appears right away as the highest bid in the marketplace, giving my order an equal footing with the other market makers.

MCI Preferred (MCICP)

Market Maker Buys			Market Maker Sells		
1	ISLD	$22\frac{9}{16}$	1	MLCO	$22\frac{5}{8}$
10	EVRN	$22\frac{1}{2}$	10	MSRO	$22\frac{11}{16}$
2	OLDE	$22\frac{3}{8}$	10	PRUS	$22\frac{3}{4}$
20	PRUS	$22\frac{5}{16}$	1	FBRC	$22\frac{3}{4}$

> This is exactly why momentum traders choose to pay more to use direct-access systems. They ensure that limit orders get reflected properly in the market.

The reason for the market maker not reflecting my limit order was simple: The market maker had no vested interest in doing so. Remember, market makers do not like taking limit orders into the marketplace because they can't make any money on them, and when they can't make any money on them, they really have no desire to help get the best possible execution.

We are to conclude from this experiment that using regular online brokers to trade the most volatile NASDAQ stocks is a recipe for disaster. *If you don't have a direct-access system, you should not trade NASDAQ stocks.* In addition, if you do choose to use an online broker, you should stick with the New York Stock Exchange stocks because the likelihood of getting a fair execution is much greater on the NYSE than it is on the NASDAQ.

For in-depth examples and information on the questionable trading practices that some online brokers engage in, consult *The Day Trader's Survival Guide Video Companion*. (See the last page of this book.)

[3]

A Momentum Trader's Diary

Momentum trading is not day trading in the true sense of the word because most positions are not held all day. Instead, in this day and age of technology, momentum traders may buy a stock, then sell it five, ten, or fifteen seconds later. In fact, if they hold it for more than a few minutes, that is considered "long term." This chapter will explain why it is so difficult to trade the NASDAQ on a second-to-second basis, and will offer tips on how to trade it profitably.

The Mind-set of the Momentum Trader

If there is one way in which to sum up the mind-set of momentum traders, it is to say that they always want to be in a strong stock in a strong market. Imagine what it would be like if, the entire time that the stock market was open, you always owned the strongest stock on the NASDAQ. This could change on a minute-to-minute basis, so always being long the strongest stock could mean having to switch into and out of fifty or a hundred different stocks throughout the day. Think of the money you could make! In theory, this is what the day trader tries to do. If you could do this, you would always be involved in the stock that, at that particular time, was surging higher. This is exactly how some momentum traders are able to make $50,000 or $100,000 in a single day, as we have seen in the newspapers.

Strong Stocks on Pullbacks

One of the things that may surprise you about successful momentum traders is that they do not recklessly chase a strong stock higher. *Instead, they wait for a strong stock's first pullback, then they buy it.* For instance, if a stock like Rambus is up 40 points on the day, but has run 10 points in the last ten minutes, day traders will not touch it until it comes in slightly, even if it runs another 20 points higher before coming in. Strong stocks always "pull in" at some point, and buying a stock at the precise moment it cannot pull in farther offers the best chance of profit.

For example, a day trader would rather buy Rambus at $300 on its first pullback of the morning than "top tick" it at $280 if it hasn't pulled in at all. Why would you rather pay $300 for a stock than $280? In a nutshell, it is a game of risk versus reward, and there is a much higher percentage play when a strong stock has given off a little bit of steam than there is when buying it on its highs of the day. This is what we mean when we say that absolute valuations mean nothing to day traders. A one-point profit is a one-point profit, regardless of whether you bought the stock at 280 and sold it at 281, or bought it at 300 and sold it at 301. What is more important is *how much risk you took in the process.*

Buying a Strong Stock When the Overall Market Turns Higher

In addition to buying strong stocks on pullbacks, the day trader also looks to buy strong stocks at that precise moment when the overall market heads higher. This is because strong stocks are more likely to head higher in a market rally than weak ones. In other words, when the market gets stronger, it is far more likely to see a stock that is up 10 points on the day rally another 2 points than to see a stock down 10 points on the day have that same 2-point rally.

The S&P Futures and the Slingshot Effect

The best way to look at this phenomenon is to think of it as a slingshot. Typically, when the market indexes turn higher, the buying pressure creates a slingshot effect in the strongest stocks. This is when you see a strong stock like Rambus shoot higher by 5 points in a matter of seconds! The day traders who are able to read this, and exploit the move, consistently make money on this kind of trade.

So what is the best way to determine whether the overall market is headed higher or lower? Day traders follow one and only one thing: the S&P futures. As a day trader, the only thing you have to know about the S&P futures, or "spus," is that they are the spark that ignites rallies in strong NASDAQ stocks. The S&P futures market is best understood as the place where large money managers put massive amounts of money to work in a very short period of time. Why do money managers park money in the S&P futures? *Because they will rally before anything else does.* If you were the head of a $50-billion-dollar mutual fund, and you wanted to take advantage of the short upsurge in the market, the easiest way to do it would be by buying S&P futures contracts.

As we have seen, momentum traders look to buy strong stocks when the overall market heads higher. But what do they do when the S&P futures are headed lower? They do the exact opposite: they look to "short" weak stocks. When you short a stock, you sell it before buying it. It is a bet that the stock is headed lower, and the lower it goes, the more profit you make. If you are a beginner, I would strongly recommend that you refrain from shorting stocks. It requires a level of skill and precision that you don't have when you start out in the game of momentum trading. In other words, you will get hurt badly if you short the wrong stock at the wrong time. There are so many opportunities in this bull market to buy strong stocks that you shouldn't consider shorting stocks until you have more experience.

The S&P Futures Voice Feed

The trading edge that comes from knowing where the S&P futures are headed is so essential that some advanced day traders (myself included) actually use a voice feed from the S&P futures pit. It is called "the spus call," and there are companies that offer this service over the Internet for about $100 per month. Basically, it is a play-by-play "call" from a trader in the futures pit that allows you to hear the movements the split second they are happening. The result? You can capitalize on movements about one to two seconds before the rest of the world even sees them. Some of the best day trading firms utilize this service in their offices, playing it over the loudspeakers all day long. For instance, a day trader will look to buy a strong stock like Redback the split-second that he hears the trader in the S&P futures pit say "buyers coming in" or "better bid . . . better bid. . . . better bid. . . ." There are enough day traders listening to this voice feed now that these volatile stocks will easily rally 2 or 3 points in less than ten seconds as a reaction to this. The day traders who trade without this service will miss the opportunity, and will inevitably be left wondering what happened as the stock bolts higher. Many of the large hedge funds, arbitrageurs, and brokerage firms have used these voice feed services for years, but thanks to the Internet, it is only recently that they have become affordable for day traders as well. (Visit my website at *www.farrell-trading.com* for an up-to-date list of providers and prices of the S&P voice service.)

Commissions Can Be a Killer

From the day trader's perspective, there are two evils that can very quietly destroy trading capital in a very short period of time: the bid-ask spread, and commissions. The first evil is one we talked about earlier: If you pay the spread on every trade, you will be out of the game fast. But the second evil, commissions, can be even more destructive. *Excessive trading is the fastest road to ruin in momentum trading.* Commissions are so dangerous because they are a hidden expense, and many day traders do not pay attention to them during the trading day. They get so caught up in the movements of the market that the 2 cents per share or the $22 per trade that they are paying seems meaningless. However, if you do fifty or a hundred trades per day, the commission bill could be in the thousands of dollars each day. As you know, you have to pay this bill regardless of whether you turn a profit or not. Always keep in the back of your mind that a break-even trade is really, on paper, a losing trade because of the commissions you pay. *You are not out to make the day trading firm rich, you are out to make yourself rich.* The high commission cost of excessive trading is yet another reason for seven out of ten day traders ultimately failing.

The Search for Telltale Signs of Strength and Weakness

In this game of finding strong stocks in strong markets, the day trader must make the distinction between a strong situation and a weak one. Even though the stock you have been trading all morning is up 10 points on the day, at any given moment conditions can change drastically. The stock you thought was strong could now be weak, and if you are slow to react to it, you will lose money. Recognizing and reacting to these changes is perhaps the most important skill a momentum trader can possess.

This is why you must have an extremely short-term perspective if you are going to make it as a momentum trader. This is also why so many momentum traders ultimately fail. These NASDAQ stocks are so volatile that, literally, one minute they could be on an up trend, and the next minute they could get caught in a downdraft. You cannot be influenced by what your opinion of the stock was even five minutes earlier. If you are on the wrong side at the wrong time, you will get steamrolled. And if you are on the right side of it, you will make money. It is that simple.

It is very important to hone the skill of reading how a stock changes from being good one second to bad the next. It is this transition that gives the day trader his best opportunity for a profitable trade: *to buy at the end of the weakness, and sell into the strength.* To shed some light on this, we will now compare how a stock changes from weak to strong in a matter of only sixty seconds.

As we will see below, when a dead stock starts showing the first signs of coming to life, that is when the day trader must jump aboard. These NASDAQ stocks move so incredibly fast that you will not have the luxury of waiting until conditions improve before trying to buy the stock. If you do, you will miss the move and it could cost you several points of lost profit. At the slightest hint of a positive change in the stock, you have to be looking to buy the stock (on the bid, of course). If you wait, it may be the difference between making $500 on the trade and losing that much.

Broadcom (BRCM)

Market Maker Buys			Market Maker Sells		
50	SBSH	183	4	MCLO	$183\frac{3}{8}$
50	NITE	183	5	DLJP	$183\frac{5}{8}$
50	COWN	183	2	ARCA	$183\frac{7}{8}$
50	MASH	183	1	ISLD	184

What makes the day trader want to buy the stock now? There are two very important things that are happening in the stock now that weren't happening in the first example. (1) Look at how many more buyers have joined the bid at 183, and (2) notice that the wall of sellers at $183\frac{3}{8}$ has disappeared. More stock willing to be bought, and less stock willing to be sold. The stock is much more likely to head higher now than it was sixty seconds earlier.

Another thing to keep in mind: If you get in the habit of paying the spread, it will destroy any realistic chance you have of making a living as a momentum trader. So when you see an opportunity to buy stock, you must try to buy it on the bid. If you are unable to buy on the bid, it may be better to just let the stock go. If you can't buy the stock on your terms, you shouldn't buy it. This is what separates successful day traders from those who are unsuccessful: the ability to refrain from making a trade. What many people new to day trading don't understand is that 90 percent of your day should be spent *watching,* not trading. Even if you miss a few good opportunities along the way, there is no harm done in missing a trade. If you have the discipline to trade only when the odds are overwhelmingly in your favor, that is what will keep you in the game for the long haul. A key component in having the discipline to refrain from trading is the ability to know when a situation is good, and when it is not.

A Very Good Situation That Turns Sour

This stock looks like a very good buy right now. Strong buying support at 103, and very few sellers up above.

Qualcomm (QCOM)

Market Maker Buys			Market Maker Sells		
20	HMQT	103	5	ISLD	$103\frac{1}{4}$
20	SBSH	103	1	ATTN	$103\frac{3}{8}$
10	MASH	103	8	SHWD	$103\frac{1}{2}$
20	NITE	$102\frac{15}{16}$	5	DAIN	$103\frac{5}{8}$

A very good situation one minute turns sour the next. Look at the wall of sellers that seem to appear from out of nowhere up at $103\frac{1}{8}$.

Market Maker Buys			Market Maker Sells		
20	HMQT	103	10	SBSH	$103\frac{1}{8}$
20	SBSH	103	50	GSCO	$103\frac{1}{8}$
10	MASH	103	40	CEUT	$103\frac{1}{8}$
20	NITE	$102\frac{15}{16}$	50	LEHM	$103\frac{1}{8}$

The Necessity of Trading with the Ebb and Flow of the Major Market Makers

Now that we have had a glimpse of how a day trader determines when to go long or short a stock, we have to take a step back and look at the bigger picture. In the earlier chapters, we painted a picture of the successful day trader as someone who trades with the ebbs and flows of the market makers, not against them. The day trader must always keep in the back of his mind that the NASDAQ market makers he is trading against, particularly those at the prestigious investment banks like Goldman Sachs, Salomon Smith Barney, Morgan Stanley, First Boston, and Merrill Lynch, are the very best, brightest, and most experienced that Wall Street has to offer.

The Food Chain

When the day trader is trying to interpret the moves of the market makers, many times it is not the movements themselves that matter. Instead, what matters more is *who* is doing the buying and selling. Wall Street is a very stratified industry, with a very long food chain. There are small firms that carry no influence, and large firms that have the power to move markets, standing side by side and trading with one another. This is the way it has always been. The firms that move markets have always been the highest on the food chain and the most respected, and they always will be. The day trader would be very wise to follow in their footsteps and mirror their actions: Buy when they are buying and sell when they are selling.

When the day trader reacts to the movements of the market makers, he needs to have a firm grasp of *who* they are. As you can see, a big part of the day trader's job is to make judgments as to which market makers are capable of moving markets, and which aren't. For instance, when the day trader sees a smaller brokerage firm, like Gruntal or Olde, bidding for "size," he is going to be less concerned than if it is one of the big investment banks like Prudential, Salomon Smith Barney, or Merrill Lynch. That is not to say that these smaller, "second tier" market makers can't move these markets around when they have a big buy or sell order. They can. It is just that they don't have the resources or the pockets that the "heavy hitters" do, so generally speaking, their presence is not going to have the same effect on the market.

Goldman Sachs as a Seller Is Enough to Scare the Daylights Out of Most Day Traders

For instance, when a company like Goldman Sachs appears as an aggressive seller, most day traders will flee the scene. There is a reason for this. A company like Goldman Sachs will steamroll you if you try to get in their way. That is why you must always treat their presence with respect. Always remember that when you are trading in the same markets they are, you are competing with powers and market forces that are far larger and more powerful than you and I.

The Heavy Hitters

Who are the heavy hitters, and how do you differentiate them from the rest of the market makers? Though the electronic trading revolution has changed the financial landscape by bringing once obscure online firms into the spotlight, it is still the old-line, New York City–based brokerage powerhouses that wield the largest sword on Wall Street. You know the names: Goldman Sachs, Merrill Lynch, Salomon Smith Barney, Morgan Stanley Dean Witter, First Boston, Prudential, J. P. Morgan, and Lehman Brothers. These heavy hitters have two things in common: (1) the deepest pockets on

Wall Street, and (2) the largest institutional clients in the world. In addition, some also boast huge retail sales forces. For instance, not only does a firm like Merrill Lynch have institutional clients, including the largest pension funds, hedge funds, and mutual funds, but it also has tens of thousands of stockbrokers within its network. Imagine how much stock can be "put away" within Merrill Lynch's system when one of their most influential analysts releases a buy recommendation.

DEEP POCKETS MOVE MARKETS

The golden rule rings true on the buy side as well: When the smart money is buying, it is time to jump aboard.

Adaptive Broadband (ADAP)

Market Maker Buys			Market Maker Sells		
30	MLCO	110	5	NITE	$110\frac{1}{4}$
30	MSCO	110	5	ATTN	$110\frac{1}{4}$
10	PRUS	110	8	SLCK	$110\frac{3}{8}$
15	SBSH	110	6	INCA	$110\frac{7}{16}$

Notice in this example that Merrill Lynch, Morgan Stanley, Prudential, and Salomon Smith Barney are all advertising themselves as buyers. These investment banks have billions of dollars of trading capital, and the biggest institutional clients in the world. When they are buying aggressively, watch out. The stock is probably headed higher.

To put this in perspective, I like to use the analogy of a big oil tanker and a lone individual on a jet ski sharing the same waterway. Look at the oil tanker as one of the large brokerage firms on Wall Street. These large brokerage firms are the ones that have the power, pockets, and resources to do whatever they want to a stock. The day trader is the jet skier who weaves in and out and rides the waves created by the oil tanker. The last thing the jet skier wants to do is move in front of the oil tanker's path. It is far easier to follow in its wake. The same is true in day trading. You don't have to lead the large market makers. Instead, you can follow the momentum that their buying and selling creates.

A NONEVENT

When a "second tier" market maker shows up as a seller, it is typically a "nonevent." Unless it is one of the powerhouse brokerage firms, the mere appearance of a smaller market maker as an aggressive seller is not going to drive the market down.

Amazon.com (AMZN)

Market Maker Buys			Market Maker Sells		
5	BEST	$80\frac{3}{8}$	30	JBOC	$80\frac{5}{8}$
5	RSSF	$80\frac{1}{4}$	10	CEUT	$80\frac{3}{4}$
5	BEST	$80\frac{1}{8}$	4	ISLD	$80\frac{7}{8}$
10	HMQT	80	3	INCA	81

In this example, just because JBOC shows up as a seller of 3,000 shares doesn't mean that the day traders will run for the hills. However, do not get the false impression that these second tier brokerage firms can't move the market if they have a big buy or sell order. They can. It is just that, from the day trader's perspective, a smaller firm's presence is not a telltale sign that the market is headed lower.

The House Always Wins

When we say in day trading that the house always wins, who is the house? On the NASDAQ, the house happens to be the "heavy hitters" we just described. These big brokerage firms control the market, and their buying and selling dictates where the stock is headed. That is why it is so important for the day trader to be keenly aware of what these big players are doing. At this point in the day, are they buying or are they selling?

The Time to Buy Is When the Heavy Hitters Switch from Net Sellers to Net Buyers

In this first example, Brocade Communications (BRCD) is not a good buy when the smart money is selling . . .

Brocade Communications (BRCD)

Market Maker Buys			Market Maker Sells		
5	ADAM	275	5	GSCO	276
10	NEED	274¼	10	MLCO	276
3	GRUN	273¾	10	MSCO	276½
9	OLDE	273	10	SBSH	276½

When the heavy hitters switch from being "net" sellers to "net" buyers, the day trader would be very wise to join them.

Market Maker Buys			Market Maker Sells		
4	SBSH	273	1	NITE	274
5	GSCO	273	3	ISLD	274½
5	MSCO	273	1	ATTN	275
5	MLCO	273	2	MASH	275½

It is very important to keep in the back of your mind that if Morgan Stanley, Merrill Lynch, and Goldman Sachs are consistently taking the other side of your trades, the odds are that you are almost certain to lose money.

Now that we have established that the key to success as a momentum trader is to follow the smart money, several questions may arise. What happens when the heavy hitters are split? What do you do when you see Goldman Sachs as a buyer, but Morgan Stanley and Merrill Lynch as sellers? Under those circumstances the answer is that you probably shouldn't trade. You should wait a few minutes, until you see a clearer picture of where the stock is headed. Remember, there is no harm done in sitting on your hands. You never want to be in a position of guessing. If you have to guess, that is not day trading. That is gambling, and gamblers do not last long in this business.

The Market Makers Do Trade Together

In the first chapter we touched upon the fact that the major market makers stay in business by selling rallies and buying dips. In a nutshell, they are net buyers on weakness and net sellers on strength. The market makers, as a group, are essentially in the business of accumulating stock on the way down and selling it on the way up. In other words, they buy the stock when no one wants it, and they sell it when everyone wants it. This is a pattern that you see over and over. The market makers, the smart money, are "in sync" with one another because they are seasoned veterans and know how to exploit the market for profit. Remember, these aren't the highest-paid traders on Wall Street for nothing. The fact that they are in tune with each other is exactly what creates the momentum in the first place. And as you know, this is the momentum that the day trader looks to follow.

But there is one problem with this equation. As day traders we do not have the deep pockets that a Lehman Brothers or a Prudential has. We don't have the luxury of having a $50-million arsenal of trading capital. This war chest serves as a cushion if the market makers happen to be on the wrong side of a trade. What happens if they buy on the way down, but the market goes against them and the stock continues to head lower? They have the buying power to purchase more stock if that is what they want to do. But the day trader can't do that. What if you have only enough money to buy 300 shares? You get one and only one shot, and there is no margin for error. That is why you have to wait until conditions are nearly perfect before placing the trade.

Are the Heavy Hitters Net Buyers?

Thankfully, there are going to be several times during the trading day when the odds will be overwhelmingly in your favor. What makes for nearly perfect conditions? How do you know when the odds are in your favor? As a rule of thumb, it is going to be those times when the heavy hitters are acting in sync as "net" buyers. There are two times when you can be reasonably sure that this occurs: (1) buying a strong stock on its first pullback, and (2) buying a strong stock when the S&P futures turn higher. This is what we will discuss next.

A Strong Stock on Its First Pullback

When the day trader buys a strong stock on its first pullback of the morning, this is the highest-percentage trade of the whole day. Why? Because it is a clear and predictable transition that the smart money makes from being "net" sellers to becoming "net" buyers. Strong stocks open high because the market makers are "net" sellers on the open. Remember, part of the responsibility of being a NASDAQ market maker is to provide liquidity to the market: to be a buyer when the market needs buyers, and to be a seller when the market needs sellers. When the whole world wants to buy stock, the market makers are forced into being the sellers of last resort. This is what we mean when we say that the market makers buy stock when no one wants it and sell stock when everyone wants it.

This is the key to buying low and selling high. Put yourself in the shoes of the head trader at Morgan Stanley or Merrill Lynch on a morning when every firm on Wall Street has a buy recommendation on Amazon.com. There will be a huge buy imbalance that must be rectified at the open of trading. As a major market maker, you are the last line of defense for this buy imbalance. The buck stops with you.

Licking Your Chops

So what do you do if the buying imbalance is so extreme that you are forced into selling 1 million shares on the open to your clients? You lick your chops and use it as an opportunity to make a huge profit at the expense of the very clients your firm claims to serve. Why do you think some NASDAQ traders get paid multimillion-dollar salaries? Because the brokerage firms employing them know just how lucrative these kinds of opportunities can be if exploited. You open the stock as high as possible, short the stock to your firm's customers, let it drop, and then minutes later you buy it back at a lower price for a nice profit.

PHASE 1: THE SEEDS OF THE SUCKER BET HAVE BEEN PLANTED

When the stock opens for trading up 20 points on good news, the market makers use the buying climax as an opportunity to sell. They either liquidate their long positions or, in most cases, use the high opening price (100) to establish a large short position.

Amazon.com (AMZN)

Market Maker Buys			Market Maker Sells		
3	ISLD	99¾	20	MASH	100
10	ATTN	99½	20	SLCK	100
4	NITE	99½	20	BEST	100
3	FBCO	99½	20	RSSF	100

By 9:30 A.M. the seeds of the sucker bet have been planted: The investing public are net buyers while the market makers are net sellers.

The Smart Money Is Selling at the Open

The market makers love this situation. They will open the stock at a price level they feel certain can't go any higher. The smart money is selling at the open. Remember the rule: *When the smart money sells, it is because the stock is probably headed lower.* That is exactly why a stock like Amazon.com, on many days, never breaks the high that it sets on the opening "print."

You must keep in mind that this is capitalism in its purest form. The market makers risk their capital to make money at the expense of the investing public. They are there to take your money, *if you let them.* Keep the sucker theme in the back of your mind. The suckers are the ones who get taken to the cleaners. Who are the suckers in this example? They are the masses of investors buying Amazon.com "at market" on the open. When the smart money is selling, it can be said that the "dumb money" is buying. How can the stock possibly trade any higher than it does during a buying climax like this one? Where does it go once all of the stock ends up in the hands of the suckers?

This is why, from the day trader's standpoint, buying on good news rarely works. It doesn't work because this is the one time that the market makers are going to force you to pay top dollar to buy the stock. Think about it. Are the market makers selling you the stock because they are stupid? Do they short-sell 1 million shares at 100 because they think it is going to trade higher than that? That is why buying on good news is perhaps the best example of a bet against the house.

The Brokerage Firms Now Have a Complete Conflict of Interest

Once the market makers sell the stock on the open, they now have a complete conflict of interest. On the one hand, their analyst just put a buy recommendation on the stock and all of their biggest clients now own it. And on the other hand, while all of the firm's clients are long the stock, the firm's trading desk is actually short the stock. This is a complete absurdity. The highest-paid analyst in the brokerage firm puts a "glowing" buy recommendation on the stock, yet the company's very own trading desk not only doesn't listen, but does the exact opposite by shorting the stock! Wouldn't you think that it would be the other way around? Shouldn't the trading desk follow the trusted advice of their "star" analyst? Shouldn't the brokerage firm put its money where its mouth is? Common sense would tell you that it should. However, it doesn't work that way on Wall Street.

By 9:31 A.M. the engines that will drive the stock lower have been put in place. The wall of sellers is forming at 100. The appearance of this wall makes it look as if the whole world is heading for the exits. The stock appears "weighed down." The market makers are doing this intentionally in the hope that this will cause the stock to drop.

Amazon.com(AMZN)

Market Maker Buys				Market Maker Sells		
5	NEED	$99\frac{5}{8}$		30	BEST	100
5	HMQT	$99\frac{9}{16}$		20	LEHM	100
5	CEUT	$99\frac{1}{2}$		20	PERT	100
5	AGIS	$99\frac{7}{16}$		30	SBSH	100

Remember, the market makers with the deepest pockets do not mind selling more stock at 100 after they open it. If they have already sold short 1 million shares at 100 on the open, what difference does it make to them to sell another 50,000 at that price afterward? They will sell as much additional stock at 100 as possible to prevent the stock from trading higher.

The market makers have a fine-tuned plan in place. If they can make the stock look weak, all of those people who bought the stock at 100 on the open may start to head for the exits if they think it is going lower. It becomes a self-fulfilling prophesy. As the stock heads lower, the selling pressure intensifies. And because the market makers are short, the lower it goes, the more money they will make.

PHASE 3: THE UNWELCOME GUEST JOINS THE FEAST

The most disliked member of Wall Street's food chain, the day trader, is right there with the brokerage firms trying to drive the stock lower.

Amazon.com (AMZN)

Market Maker Buys			Market Maker Sells		
5	NEED	$99\frac{5}{8}$	20	ISLD	100
5	HMQT	$99\frac{9}{16}$	20	INCA	100
5	CEUT	$99\frac{1}{2}$	30	BEST	100
5	AGIS	$99\frac{7}{16}$	30	LEHM	100

Look at the ECNs that have joined in the wall of sellers at 100: Island (ISLD) and Instinet (INCA). These are not market makers, they are day traders, and they are after the same exact thing that the market makers are: They want to manipulate the stock lower.

The Day Traders Join the Fray

There is another dynamic going on here as well. The market makers are not the only ones involved in this game. Guess who else is trying to drive the stock lower? The day traders! Remember the three out of ten day traders we talked about who consistently make money? They don't make money day in and day out by letting opportunities slip by. The most aggressive of them are right there shorting the stock with the market makers on the open at 100. Once the day traders get short the stock, they aid the market makers in attempting to make the stock look weak.

PHASE 4: THE DOMINO EFFECT BEGINS

The dangerous thing about the presence of the day traders is that they will not waste any time up at 100. One by one, the most aggressive of them will start jumping ahead of the market makers and lowering their offers to $99\frac{3}{4}$. This begins a domino effect as the day traders start underoffering each other.

Amazon.com (AMZN)

Market Maker Buys			Market Maker Sells		
5	NEED	$99\frac{5}{8}$	10	ISLD	$99\frac{3}{4}$
5	HMQT	$99\frac{9}{16}$	10	INCA	$99\frac{3}{4}$
5	CEUT	$99\frac{1}{2}$	30	BEST	100
5	AGIS	$99\frac{7}{16}$	30	LEHM	100

The wall of sellers at 100 now becomes a wall of sellers at $99\frac{3}{4}$, and dropping fast. The day traders go "low offer" and the market makers are quick to follow. The wheels are in motion and the momentum is starting to pick up. This is when the stock really begins to head south.

The Day Traders Are Bluffing

It is essential that you understand the trading psychology the day traders are employing here. Remember, day traders do not have the deep pockets that the market makers have. Once they have established a short position at 100, the last thing any day trader wants to do is add to the position at worse prices. In other words, just because you see INCA and ISLD aggressively offering stock for sale at $99\frac{3}{4}$ *it doesn't mean that they actually want the stock to trade*. They are advertising to the market that they are sellers, but in reality these day traders are hoping and praying that no one takes their stock. It is a bluff, a ploy to make the stock look weak. This kind of thing goes on all the time, and you have to be ready for it. The problem is that the investing public doesn't even know it.

PHASE 5: A HOT KNIFE THROUGH BUTTER

The investing public falls right into the trap that the day traders and the market makers have set. When the stock appears to be under selling pressure, the investing public gets nervous. And when they get nervous, they start heading for the exits.

Amazon.com (AMZN)

Market Maker Buys   Market Maker Sells

5	GRUN	99¼	20	ISLD	99⅜
5	AGIS	99⅛	30	INCA	99⅜
5	SLCK	99	10	GSCO	99½
5	COWN	98⅞	10	MLCO	99½

Some of the stock that was bought by the investing public at 100 on the open now comes back into the market in the form of panic selling, sending the stock into a mini-freefall in a matter of seconds. The stock trades through each price level like a hot knife through butter, as the bids at 99⅝, 99⁹⁄₁₆, 99½, and 99⁷⁄₁₆ disintegrate.

Notice the next level of bids below 99⁷⁄₁₆. There is no real buying support from the market makers. This is further exaggerated by the day traders, who keep underoffering each other and weighing down the stock. At this point neither the market makers nor the day traders have any inclination to support the stock. They will wait until it trades lower before becoming buyers.

The Investing Public Have Now Become Net Sellers

There are two very important things going on right here: (1) the investing public, who were net buyers on the open, have now become net sellers, and (2) because of this, the market makers are not supporting the stock with large bids. The investing public couldn't buy enough of it when it opened at 100, and now, minutes later, they can't seem to sell it fast enough. This is the self-fulfilling prophesy we talked about earlier. The investing public becomes their own worst enemy during panic selling, and the market makers know it. This will continue for several minutes, and will reach a climax when the selling is most intense. When this happens, guess who begins to buy back the stock?

PHASE 6: THE MARKET MAKERS START SUCKING UP THE STOCK LIKE A VACUUM CLEANER

Once the stock has fallen down to 99, the market makers turn on a dime and quickly become aggressive buyers. Like a vacuum cleaner, they "suck" up all of the stock that the investing public is dumping. Look at the wall of bids that show up at 99.

Amazon.com (AMZN)

Market Maker Buys			Market Maker Sells		
20	GSCO	99	5	MASH	$99\frac{1}{8}$
20	BEST	99	5	NITE	$99\frac{3}{16}$
20	LEHM	99	5	HRZQ	$99\frac{1}{4}$
20	MSCO	99	5	HMQT	$99\frac{5}{16}$

When the stock opened, the market makers sold into the buying climax at 100. Now the market makers are buying into the selling climax at 99. The second phase of the sucker bet has been put in place. The stock is now headed higher.

You will now see why buying a strong stock on the pullback is the best trade of the day. Once the brokerage firms bring the stock in far enough, they become aggressive buyers. Why do they suddenly go from being sellers to being buyers? Because they are short the stock at 100, and they need to buy it back at a lower price to lock in the profit. Imagine shorting 100,000 shares at 100 and buying it back three minutes later at 99. That is a $100,000 profit, the whole reason for this drama playing out the way it does.

PHASE 7: THE FEEDING FRENZY CREATES A SLINGSHOT EFFECT

The day traders do not jump right in with the market makers. Instead, they let the "deep pockets" absorb the selling pressure first. When it looks as if the stock can't come in any more, the day traders jump all over it and bombard it with buy orders. The buying pressure by both the market makers and the day traders completely overwhelms the stock. In a matter of only a few seconds, the feeding frenzy sends the stock back toward 100, as if it had been shot out of a slingshot.

Amazon.com (AMZN)

Market Maker Buys			Market Maker Sells		
20	ISLD	$99\frac{1}{8}$	5	NITE	$99\frac{3}{16}$
20	INCA	$99\frac{1}{8}$	5	HRZG	$99\frac{1}{4}$
20	GSCO	99	5	HMQT	$99\frac{5}{16}$
20	BEST	99	5	COWN	$99\frac{3}{8}$

This is why buying a strong stock on the pullback is the highest-percentage trade of the entire day. Any day trader who is able to anticipate this move and buy stock with the market makers at 99 or $99\frac{1}{8}$ will probably be selling the stock thirty seconds later up at $99\frac{3}{4}$ or higher. If you have enough capital to buy 1,000 shares, that is your $750 or $1,000 profit before 9:32 A.M. Not a bad way to start the trading day.

Are the Day Traders "in Cahoots" with the Market Makers in Manipulating the Stock?

It may seem, at first glance, that the day traders are "in cahoots" with the market makers in inflating and deflating the stock price. This could not be farther from the truth. You may be surprised to know the main reason for the stock shooting higher, as if it had been shot out of a slingshot: It is because the marker makers can actually be in a state of panic themselves. The last thing any brokerage firm wants is for the day traders to start running the stock higher before the market makers can cover their short positions. If this does happen, a nice profit for the market makers could easily turn into a heavy loss. Think about it from the standpoint of being short 100,000 shares at 100. What happens if the stock moves from 99 to 100 to 101 so fast that you are not able to cover your short? Your $100,000 paper profit at 99 could become a $100,000 *realized loss* at 101! This is why the market makers treat the day traders with a certain degree of respect.

Day Traders Let the Market Makers Do the Dirty Work First

Did you notice that, in this example, the day traders became more aggressive buyers than the market makers? The day traders were also more aggressive on the sell side. There is a pattern developing here: *The day traders who make consistent money always seem to be one step ahead of the market makers.* It is almost as if they let the market makers do the dirty work for them. The day traders sit and watch while the first wave of market makers use their deep pockets to absorb the selling pressure. At the precise moment the market makers have succeeded in preventing the stock from falling farther, the day traders run ahead of the market makers, grabbing all of the cheap stock for themselves before the market makers can get their hands on it.

From the day trader's standpoint, buying a strong stock on the pullback is a great trading strategy because there is not that much risk involved. *The stock can't go any lower because it has already fallen!* In other words, the move lower is over. Why has the stock finished falling? The simple answer is that the market makers are now supporting the stock, when sixty seconds earlier they weren't. This ebb and flow can be summed up in three moves:

1. The market makers sold at 100 while the investing public bought at 100.

2. Immediately after the investing public bought stock, the market makers and the day traders made the stock look weak, which fooled the investing public into panic selling.

3. Once the panic selling reached a climax, and the stock dropped a full point in a matter of one or two minutes, the market makers started buying aggressively. The day traders reacted to this by joining the buying frenzy. Thus, the market makers and the day traders made money two ways—on the way down and back on the way up—by selling short at 100, covering on the way down to 99, getting long at the bottom, and selling into the updraft that followed.

This kind of ebb and flow is repeated over and over throughout the day. There is one consistent theme: The market makers sell when the investing public buys, and the market makers buy when the investing public sells. The day trader who consistently does the same makes very good money. The reason for this being such a great trade is that major market forces seem to all collide at once to create this opportunity. Think about it from the day trader's standpoint: Imagine how profitable it is to make money two ways on this trade. First on the way down from 100 to 99, and then on the way back up from 99 to 100.

Are the Market Makers Net Long or Net Short?

This kind of example sheds light on one of the most profound and misunderstood aspects of momentum trading. What really moves stock prices? The answer may surprise you. The number one factor in determining if a NASDAQ stock is headed higher or lower is not charts, graphs, and research but, instead, whether the market makers, as a group, are "net long" or "net short." If they are net long, the market makers will do everything in their power to guide the stock higher, and if they are short, they will try by all means necessary to manipulate it lower.

We need only review what happened here to prove that fact. What caused the stock to drop like a rock, from 100 to 99, in the minutes after it opened? Did the chart indicate that it was a sell? Did an analyst come out and say that it was overpriced? No, the analysts were actually recommending the stock and the chart probably looked "bullish." It dropped because the market makers were short the stock and had no financial interest in trying to support it. The farther it dropped, the more money they stood to make.

Playing with Fire: A Few Words on Trading IPOs

No day trading book would be complete without touching briefly upon the world of initial public offerings, or IPOs. If there is one thing I can impress upon you, as far as IPOs go, DON'T TRADE THEM! You are asking for trouble if you do. They are too volatile and they are not worth the risk. This is by far the most volatile segment of the NASDAQ market. It is not uncommon to see an IPO open for trading on its first day 100 points above its offering price! You may get lucky and double your money in twenty minutes if you catch a good one, but you could also lose an entire month's profit in an afternoon.

The problem with trading a high-flying IPO is that it is a bet outside the parameters of supply and demand. The stock could open at 100, go up 80 points, and then immediately drop 40 points in the minutes that follow. Or it could open at 100 and then go straight to 150. In other words, there is no way to tell what an IPO is going to do after it opens for trading. It is an outright gamble, and gambling has no place in the day trader's world.

The Pump and Dump

There is no better example of the dangers of trading initial public offerings than MP3, which had its initial public offering on July 21, 1999. The offering price on the stock was in the mid-20s, but when the IPO finally started trading in the secondary market, it opened over 100!

MP3 (MPPP) on July 21, 1999
12 noon—stock opens up around 100
12:05 P.M.—stock immediately drops 10 points to 90
12:15 P.M.—stock is down over 20 points from its opening print, trading at 81 and falling fast
12:25 P.M.—not even thirty minutes after it opens at 100, the stock is trading at 77
1:07 P.M.—stock has fallen over 30 points in thirty-seven minutes, and is trading down at 70!

The peculiar thing is that when it opened at 12 noon, it dropped like a rock! By 1:20 P.M. only eighty minutes later, the stock was trading at 65, down 35 points from its opening price. At one point, the stock was so volatile, and the supply and demand so distorted, that the stock was actually trading simultaneously at 104 and 92! How can you possibly make money trading a stock that is trading all over the map, at two different prices, 12 points apart, at the same time?

Finding Temporary "Cracks" in the Supply and Demand

It is time to switch gears and look at another trading strategy in the game of momentum trading. On the NASDAQ, the momentum trader does not always need to find a strong stock in order to make money. There are going to be times when quick money can be made regardless of whether the stock is trending higher or lower. These opportunities arise because of inefficiencies in the NASDAQ's market-maker system. What do we mean by "inefficiencies"? We mean temporary "cracks" in the supply and demand of the stock.

Finding and exploiting these temporary "cracks" in supply and demand is an incredibly lucrative proposition. This is because there are actually pockets of "free money" that exist, and these kinds of trades seek to capture it. What are pockets of free money? Simply put, they are spaces or gaps between where the market makers on NASDAQ Level II happen to be at a given time. A gap exists only because a market maker is temporarily out of place. These cracks are extremely easy to spot, but more difficult to actually exploit because you are competing against everyone else to be the first on the scene. The reality is that many of these free-money opportunities may last only five or ten seconds before they are exploited. In other words, everyone else watching the stock sees them as well. Let's look at an example.

POCKETS OF "FREE MONEY"

Which market maker is out of place? NITE at 123. Look at the wide gap between bids: NITE is bidding 123, but the next highest bid is MASH at 121¾.

Inktomi (INKT)

Market Maker Buys   *Market Maker Sells*

3	NITE	123	5	DLJP	123⅛
10	MASH	121¾	5	COWN	123⅛
10	ISLD	121¾	10	INCA	123⅛
10	ATTN	121¹¹⁄₁₆	10	RSSF	123¼

> Why is NITE out of place? He should not have to pay 123 to buy stock. He could probably bid 122 and still buy it. That is an inefficiency that the market will quickly correct by sending the stock lower. The day trader must look to exploit this aberration before it disappears.

Now that we have isolated and identified a pocket of "free money" in Inktomi, the next step is taking advantage of it. What good does it do to spot the inefficiency if you are not able to exploit it? This "crack" in supply and demand can be exploited in only one way: by shorting stock to NITE at 123, and then buying it back down at 121¾. If this is done successfully, on 300 shares you are looking at a $375 profit.

The day trader is able to capture the free money by taking advantage of the fact that NITE is "out of place." NITE is sticking its neck out and over-bidding for stock at 123. The "free money" trade is a bet that the stock is headed lower. Whoever can sell short to NITE first wins the free-money prize. Once the bid is out of the way, and the day trader is short 300 shares at 123, he then needs to "cover," or buy back the stock, at a lower price to close the trade out for a profit.

CAPTURING $375

Inktomi (INKT)

Market Maker Buys			Market Maker Sells		
3	NITE	123	5	DLJP	123⅛
10	MASH	121¾	5	COWN	123⅛
10	ISLD	121¾	10	INCA	123⅛
10	ATTN	121¹¹⁄₁₆	10	RSSF	123¼

Once NITE is out of the way, the stock will naturally drift down to the next highest bid, which is 121¾. The day trader should look to buy back stock in the area of 121¾. By shorting stock at 123, and covering it at 121¾, the day trader makes $375 (on 300 shares). The irony is that this profit was in no way the result of a bullish or a bearish bet on the stock. Instead, it was made at the expense of a market maker (NITE) who was in the wrong place at the wrong time.

Profiting at the Market Maker's Expense

This is one of the rare cases in which the day trader can profit at the expense of one of the market makers. Think about it. The day trader sold short at 123 and bought the stock back at 121¾. If the day trader was able to immediately buy stock at 121¾ (to cover the short), what was the market maker thinking by bidding for stock at 123 when he probably could have bought the stock more cheaply? Wouldn't you think that the market maker is savvy enough to know that he didn't have to pay 123 to buy the stock? The answer is that the market maker is obviously not stupid. He was probably carrying a customer order into the marketplace. It is not going to be that often that these market makers are "off their game," but when they are, you must attack. If you don't, someone else will.

The day trader is not only going to be confronted with a "crack" in supply and demand on the bid side of the market. In the last example, because the "gap" between market makers was on the buyer's side of the market, the profitable trade was a bet that the stock was headed lower. We are now going to look at the same situation, but in reverse.

A MARKET MAKER OUT OF PLACE

When the market maker who is "out of place" is on the sell side of the market, the free-money trade is a bet that the stock is headed higher.

CNET (CNET)

Market Maker Buys			Market Maker Sells		
5	SELZ	70	3	PIPR	$70\frac{1}{16}$
5	MONT	$69\frac{7}{8}$	5	HRZG	$70\frac{5}{8}$

5	LEHM	$69\frac{3}{4}$		10	NITE	$70\frac{3}{4}$
5	PRUS	$69\frac{5}{8}$		6	INCA	71

Look at PIPR at $70\frac{1}{16}$. He is "off his game" because he is selling way too cheaply. In other words, he is leaving money on the table. He could probably get $70\frac{5}{8}$ or more for his stock. A day trader will profit at PIPR's expense by lifting his stock at $70\frac{1}{16}$, and immediately reselling it at a higher price, probably $70\frac{5}{8}$.

Kill or Be Killed

In this chapter we have begun to see how momentum trading is a "kill or be killed" game. Always keep in the back of your mind that this is capitalism. Everyone, from the market makers to other day traders, is out to take *your* money. That is the only reason for money being put at risk in the first place. If you are successful, it is because you were able to take other people's money from them. And if you fail, it is only because someone else was able to profit at your expense. That is the nature of the markets. What these examples teach us is that those with the deepest pockets have the power to move the market anytime they want to, even if that means manipulating stock prices to do it. Knowing the tricks and strategies that the market makers use to manipulate the markets is the first step in being able to exploit them. That is what the next chapter details.

For an in-depth explanation plus examples of NASDAQ momentum trading strategies, consult *The Day Trader's Survival Guide Video Companion.*

4

Instigating the Day Trader Stampede: How the Market Makers Manipulate Stock Prices

In the "kill or be killed" world of momentum trading, the market makers on the NASDAQ will do everything in their power to prevent the day traders from being profitable, even if it means stretching the rules of fair play. Any trader who thinks that the NASDAQ market is fair will quickly learn that it is anything but.

If you are in this business long enough, you will probably get a hint of the feeling of animosity that day traders have for the market makers on the NASDAQ. The funny thing about this hatred is that it is strictly a NASDAQ phenomenon. Generally speaking, day traders do not feel the same hatred and mistrust for the specialists on the New York Stock Exchange that they do for the NASDAQ market makers. The irony in all of this is that even with this level of animosity, the majority of day traders still choose to trade the NASDAQ over the NYSE. Does that tell us something about the nature of the NASDAQ market? Can we conclude anything from this level of mistrust?

As we have said earlier, the NASDAQ market has serious flaws that the New York Stock Exchange does not have. The rules of the NASDAQ allow the market makers to get away with far more "questionable" trading practices than the specialists on the New York Stock Exchange ever could. In fact, these questionable trading practices are so unfair that, in some situations, it makes it all but impossible for the day trader to be profitable.

One of the first steps toward profitable momentum trading is knowing when the market makers are serious and when they are bluffing. Much of your day will be spent trying to make sense of the mixed signals and the smoke and mirrors that the market makers create. *Markets do get manipulated*, and if you don't have an understanding of how it is done, you will inevitably be on the wrong side of it. As a result, you will become one of its victims and will lose money while others profit at your expense.

To set the background for this chapter, let's look at an analogy not from Wall Street, but from Main Street. Imagine that you own a small hardware store. You have 100 lawnmowers left from last year that you cannot sell. What is the best way to move this inventory? When customers walk into your store, is it more effective to have all 100 lawnmowers out in the showroom with a for sale sign on each one? Or do you keep just one in the showroom and the other ninety-nine in storage where no one can see them?

Imagine that every customer who comes into your hardware store sees just one lawnmower in the showroom with a sign attached to it reading "50 Percent Sale—Last One in Stock." The customers will have no idea that there are ninety-nine more of same lawnmower sitting in the hardware store's basement collecting dust. The result? The customers will be inclined to grab it, thinking that it is the last one. When the customer buys the lawnmower, you simply bring another one up from the basement and repeat the process until all 100 are liquidated.

It comes down to simple supply and demand. If you need to move inventory, the most effective way to do it is to fool the buyers into thinking that there is much less for sale than there actually is. You may be surprised to know that the same thing is true in the world of stock trading. Think of the day trader as the "sucker" who walks into the hardware store, and think of the market maker as the hardware store owner. Keep this theme in the back of your mind as we delve into the mechanics of market manipulation.

The Market Maker's Dilemma

The dilemma that you, as the hardware store owner, faced in the last example is not that much different from what the market makers face every single day. To understand market manipulation and why the market makers do it, you must put yourself in their shoes. As we saw in the last chapter, the market makers assigned to trading the most volatile NASDAQ stocks face many challenges and risks that no other traders on Wall Street have to face, including the specialists on the New York Stock Exchange.

We saw how the mere appearance of Goldman Sachs, Morgan Stanley, or Merrill Lynch as a seller can send immediate shock waves through the thinnest of stocks. What do you do if you are a market maker who has to unload a large block of stock? How do you even begin to sell stock without tipping off the day traders to the fact that you are a seller? Imagine a stock like VerticalNet (VERT), which is so thin that a 2,000-share sell order can cause the stock to drop 2 full points in a matter of seconds. What does a brokerage firm do when they have to sell 10,000 or 20,000 shares?

From the last chapter you have seen what happens when one of the large brokerage firms advertises itself to the market as a seller. As a market maker, how can you possibly "show your hand" to the market without becoming your own worst enemy? This is a very serious problem for the market makers. The day traders have completely interfered with the ability of the large firms to buy and sell stock, to such a degree that it has changed the way the market makers do business. No matter how badly Goldman Sachs or Merrill Lynch may want to sell stock, they can no longer advertise it to the market. If they do, they will shoot themselves in the foot. The market will drop before they can get any stock sold.

Remember when we said earlier that, as a general rule of thumb, you do not want to get into the habit of being on the wrong side of the "smart money," or betting against the house? The wisdom of the market says that if Goldman Sachs or Morgan Stanley is willing to sell stock, you can expect that the stock is probably headed lower, not higher. With this in mind, it must be said that the reason the "smart money" is smart in the first place is because the market makers are well aware of their own ability and their influence on the market. Did the head NASDAQ trader at Merrill Lynch get to where he is by being an idiot? Would he be entrusted with millions of dollars of the firm's trading capital if he didn't know how to handle a large sell order or, even more so, if he didn't know the effect his presence had on day traders?

The point here is that the market makers know exactly what kind of effect their buy or sell orders have on the market. It is not a surprise to Goldman Sachs that the stock goes lower just because they show up as a seller. The conclusion that I hope you draw is that these market makers are not stupid. They know exactly what they are doing *even when you think they don't*. When a large brokerage firm decides to advertise itself as a seller, you can bet the farm on the fact that it is fully aware of the ramifications of its actions.

If a market maker knows that all it has to do to drive a stock into the ground is to show up as a seller, couldn't the maker use that as a tool when it wants the stock to go lower? What if it could turn the tables on the day traders by "bluffing" and pretending to be a seller when it is not? Imagine the advantage that the market makers would have over the investing public if they could make a stock go higher or lower *at will*. This is exactly what goes on every single day on the NASDAQ.

Due to the sensitive nature of this material, from this point forward we are not going to mention any specific market makers by name. It is not my intention here to point the finger at market makers who engage in market manipulation, and, in fairness, not all market makers engage in these practices. I only write this to warn the day trader that these kinds of things do occasionally occur when you trade NASDAQ stocks, and you must prepare yourself accordingly. In these examples of market manipulation, the firm doing the manipulation will always be referred to as a "large brokerage firm" or as XXXX.

To gain a better understanding of this, let's look at a realistic scenario. Imagine that you are the head trader of a large brokerage firm and you have to cover a substantial short position (100,000 shares) in a volatile stock like Yahoo! (YHOO). To make matters worse, you have to close the position by 4 P.M. today because your firm's analyst has advised you to be "flat" going into the company's earnings announcement. This means you have to buy back 100,000 shares and, as you know, the last outcome you want when short is for the stock to trade higher.

For this reason the worst thing you can do is advertise to the market that you urgently need to buy stock. *You cannot show strength*. If you do the day traders will make it all but impossible for you to buy back your 100,000 shares without sending the stock soaring higher and inflicting heavy losses on you in the process. Instead, you must do the exact opposite: *You must show weakness.* You appear as a seller when, in fact, you are a buyer. The result? You disguise your buying as selling. You make the stock look weak, which brings out sellers. When the sellers come out, you "snap up" all of their stock at lower prices.

The ECNs Are Anonymous

It is important to note that this kind of market manipulation can go on because the electronic communications networks (ECNs) are anonymous. When the investing public sees Instinet (INCA) on the bid, most people would assume that it is a day trader, not an institutional buyer. But it is only a guess because there is no way to tell for sure. These ECNs have become a very popular trading vehicle for firms with deep pockets because ECNs are completely anonymous. You don't know who is doing the buying and selling. This has become a very effective tool when the market makers need to buy or sell a large block of stock and they don't want the whole world knowing what they are doing.

The First Premise of Market Manipulation

The easiest way for a market maker to buy a large block of stock is to make the market look weak. You must be aware of the fact that the market makers can be bluffing: They can disguise themselves as buyers to hide the fact that they are, in fact, sellers, and they can act like sellers when they are really aggressive buyers.

There is another variation of this trade that plays itself out on the NASDAQ every single day. Like the previous example, our market maker is an aggressive buyer in disguise. However, unlike the first scenario, instead of buying the stock through an ECN, this time the market maker will buy the stock "head on." Our market maker will do this by fooling the day traders into thinking he is only a small buyer when, in fact, he is buying everything in sight.

The strategy is simple: Our market maker draws hundreds of day traders into opening a position, and then forces them to close the position seconds later at a loss. How does he draw them in? *By manipulating the market!* What the market makers are counting on is the fact that day traders often act on impulse. They are "skittish," and as such they will enter, exit, or reverse a position in the blink of an eye. When the market makers can facilitate these movements, the results to day traders can be devastating.

In a matter of seconds, the market makers have the ability to instigate massive day trader stampedes into or out of the most volatile stocks. These split-second day trader stampedes have the potential to make the market makers tremendous amounts of money in a very short time, if they are positioned to take advantage of the movement. The market makers are fully aware of this dynamic, and will attempt to force the hand of nervous day traders at every chance they get.

Dangling the Carrot

One of the easiest and most deceptive ways in which the market makers will attempt to instigate a day trader stampede is by something I call "dangling the carrot." Let us see how this three-step drama unfolds, and the strategy plays out in a situation that day traders face over and over. The stock we will use for the example is DoubleClick (DCLK).

PHASE 1: A TOKEN BID SETS THE TRAP

The scenario of dangling the carrot is very simple: The market maker (XXXX) sets the trap by showing a small bid at the precise moment the stock appears to be heading lower.

DoubleClick (DCLK)

Market Maker Buys			Market Maker Sells		
1	XXXX	100	10	RSSF	$100\frac{1}{8}$
4	NITE	$99\frac{5}{8}$	8	COWN	$100\frac{1}{8}$
5	MSCO	$99\frac{1}{2}$	5	GRUN	$100\frac{1}{8}$
1	REDI	$99\frac{1}{2}$	3	BRUT	$100\frac{1}{8}$

The market maker, XXXX, shows a "token bid" for 100 shares at $100. XXXX is sticking its neck out on a stock that looks very weak. Notice that the next highest bid is $\frac{3}{8}$th of a point lower, at $99\frac{5}{8}$. Even worse, you have a wall of sellers at $100\frac{1}{8}$. Day traders would interpret this one and only one way: The smart money is selling and the stock is about to tank. In other words, get short or head for the exits!

At first glance XXXX appears to be "off its market." Why would it want to buy 100 shares at 100 when it could probably buy it down at 99⅝ instead? In reality, the market maker knows exactly what it is doing. Its intention is to dangle the carrot to entice greedy day traders, who think the stock is headed lower, to hit its bid at 100 before it disappears. The market maker is banking on one fact: *that it is not just going to be one day trader who attempts to sell stock to it at 100.*

When there is the sense that easy money can be made, the masses of day traders will quickly attack the weakest link in the food chain. In this case, the weakest link is the market maker who appears to be blatantly "out of place." XXXX will get bombarded with sell orders by day traders all hoping to be that lucky first and only one to hit this 100-share bid before it disappears and the stock heads lower.

PHASE 2: THE MARKET MAKER "SUCKS UP" THE STOCK

The short selling stampede begins as the day traders, sensing the easy money and a great profit opportunity, trip over each other to "hit the bid" at 100.

DoubleClick (DCLK)

Market Maker Buys			Market Maker Sells		
1	XXXX	100	10	RSSF	100⅛
4	NITE	99⅝	8	COWN	100⅛
5	MSCO	99½	5	GRUN	100⅛
1	REDI	99½	3	BRUT	100⅛

But what happens next is classic market manipulation. Like a vacuum cleaner, XXXX sucks up every last share that can be sold to it. The onslaught of day trader sell orders is met head-on by the market maker, and it is not just "filling" the 100 shares that it advertised. Instead, the market maker ends up buying thousands and thousands of shares from this bombardment of day trader sell orders.

The Large Brokerage Firm Stays on the Bid and Catches the Day Traders Off Guard

Much to the horror of the day traders, several seconds go by and our market maker stays on the bid. This catches the day traders off guard. Why hasn't XXXX filled the order and dropped? The market maker was only supposed to buy 100 shares. Every last day trader now short the stock is thinking the same exact thing: The XXXX bid at 100 should have been filled by now and the stock should be trading down at 99⅝. But *it is not!*

THE PRINTS DO NOT LIE

Concerned by the fact that the bid at 100 hasn't disappeared, day traders begin to check the prints to see what is going on.

12:10:15	100	100	12:10:15	100	100
12:10:15	100	100	12:10:15	100	100
12:10:15	100	100	12:10:15	100	100
12:10:15	100	100	12:10:15	100	100
12:10:15	100	100	12:10:15	100	100
12:10:15	100	100	12:10:15	100	100
12:10:15	100	100	12:10:15	100	100
12:10:15	100	100	12:10:15	100	100

As the prints indicate, there is a tremendous amount of trading activity occurring at $100, and *it is all in 100-share lots!* The day traders begin to conclude that our market maker is buying much more stock at $100 than the 100 shares it had first advertised. The day traders begin to sense that they have been played!

There is an old rule in day trading that states, "When something is supposed to happen and it doesn't, then it is probably time to head for the exits." Put yourself in the shoes of all of the nervous day traders who are now short the stock at 100. The bid was supposed to disappear. Our market maker should be out of the picture, and the stock should be trading down at 99⅝. The longer it stays at 100, the more nervous the day trader will become. The stock *should* fall, but it isn't.

The Truth Comes Out: Our Market Maker Is an Aggressive Buyer

The last phase of this drama unfolds when the market maker puts the nail in the coffin. XXXX knows full well that hundreds of day traders are now short the stock (they all became short the stock seconds earlier by selling it to the market maker at 100, and as you know, XXXX graciously bought every last share). The market maker also knows that the day traders are beginning to get nervous because the stock has absorbed so much selling pressure and has not budged.

PHASE 3: THE NAIL IN THE COFFIN

After buying thousands and thousands of shares at 100, our market maker will now show its hand—it is truly an aggressive buyer. And the clincher is that the bid is no longer for 100 shares. Instead, it is for 5,000 shares!

DoubleClick (DCLK)

Market Maker Buys			Market Maker Sells		
50	XXXX	100¹⁄₁₆	10	RSSF	100⅛
4	NITE	99⅝	8	COWN	100⅛
5	MSCO	99½	5	GRUN	100⅛
1	REDI	99½	3	BRUT	100⅛

XXXX is now flexing its muscle and telling the world one thing: It will "load the boat"—it will buy all the stock it can get its hands on. As far as the day traders are concerned, this is *game over!*

In much the same manner as the market maker instigating a short selling stampede seconds earlier, the market maker will now initiate a buying stampede that will bury the day traders alive. And the irony is that it is done in the reverse fashion this time. The market maker bought a large block of stock at $100 when the day traders thought it was only willing to buy 100 shares. Now, instead of disappearing, XXXX does the exact opposite. It raises its bid to $100\frac{1}{16}$!

Instigating a Short Squeeze and Panic Buying

The thousands of day traders who fell for the trap are now in a state of panic as they interpret what XXXX has done. In the seconds that follow, fear and confusion begin to settle in as the traders quietly wonder just how high our market maker will take the stock. The most experienced of day traders begin to think of the worst-case scenarios. Does XXXX now know something about the stock that no one else knows? Is there news out on the stock? Is an analyst saying something bullish that we don't know about?

PHASE 4: A SHORT-COVERING PANIC

One by one, the day traders begin to scramble to "cover their shorts," and in the process, become their own worst enemies as they trip over each other to chase the stock higher.

DoubleClick (DCLK)

Market Maker Buys			Market Maker Sells		
20	ISLD	$100\frac{1}{4}$	10	XXXX	$100\frac{1}{2}$
20	INCA	$100\frac{1}{4}$	5	SHWD	$100\frac{5}{8}$
20	MASH	$100\frac{1}{8}$	5	PIPR	$100\frac{3}{4}$
20	GRUN	$100\frac{1}{8}$	5	DLJP	$100\frac{7}{8}$

The result? The bidding war and the panic buying by the day traders causes the stock to burst higher, to $100\frac{1}{2}$ or 101 in a matter of only a few seconds.

Unable to buy stock at 100¼, this short squeeze forces day traders to pay the spread and lift offers to buy back stock. And there is some irony in this tale. Guess who is there to sell thousands of shares into this "short squeeze," up at 100½? You guessed it: the same market maker that was aggressively buying thousands of shares ½ point cheaper several seconds earlier—XXXX.

The Market Maker Finally Reveals His Poker Hand

The wisdom in this kind of scenario is that it shows that market makers will reveal their intentions to the market only when it is in their best interests to do so: *after the fact.* The day traders learned the hard way that XXXX was an aggressive buyer only after it was way too late. This example proves one of the mottos of day trading: The market maker will often use smoke and mirrors to achieve its objective. And, as you know, that is exactly what it did.

So the million-dollar question then becomes: Why dangle the carrot? Why show a bid for 100 shares when your intention is to buy much more than that? The answer is that by bidding for only 100 shares, our market maker was able to buy far more stock than if it had shown its bid for more. Its actions brought out sellers looking to make a quick buck. Had it bid for more than 100 shares, those in the market might have sensed that it had more on its mind than just buying 100. Instead of trying to sell, the hundreds of day traders might have bombarded the stock with buy orders, driving the price higher before XXXX could have bought any stocks. Doing so would have made the market maker its own worst enemy.

This example also sheds some light on how dangerous it is to compete with someone who has unlimited trading capital and deep pockets. As we have just seen, the large brokerage firms have the buying power to "move markets" whenever they want to. This is what we mean when we say that you can get steamrolled if you get in their way. And, as you know, the day trader will not have the luxury of knowing this until it is way too late. This is one of the perils that confronts the day trader each and every day.

There is another aspect of this trade worth mentioning. There was nothing unethical or immoral about the way in which the market was manipulated by our market maker. It was simply exploiting a loophole in the rules that govern the trading of NASDAQ stocks. The weapon in XXXX's arsenal was the arcane rule on the NASDAQ that makes it perfectly legal, as a market maker, to buy 10,000 shares even if your "quoted market" only advertises to the public that you are a buyer of 100.

In my opinion, that is a form of market manipulation that misleads the investing public, and thus serves to undermine confidence in the NASDAQ. Any system that allows the market makers to conceal the "real" supply and demand from the investing public does not serve the public well. This drives home one of this book's major themes: *When the true supply and demand in the stock is intentionally manipulated, or hidden from sight by a market maker, it puts the day trader and the investing public at a severe disadvantage.*

How is it fair that a market maker is able to buy 10,000 shares when only advertising to the market that it is a buyer of 100? Common sense would tell you that if the NASDAQ market was truly "fair," anyone who wanted to buy 10,000 shares ought to be required to show that 10,000-share bid to the marketplace. That way there would be no chance of market manipulation, and day traders like you and I would not be caught on the short end of the stick. Think about it for a moment. If you saw a 10,000-share bid instead of a 100-share bid, would you react differently? Would you still be inclined to short the stock? The answer is no.

Even worse, if you or I wanted to buy 10,000 shares, we would have to display the whole 10,000-share bid to the marketplace in order to do so. Yet it is perfectly legal for the market maker to display only 100 shares and accomplish the same goal. Even in this day and age, it proves that the market makers have certain "luxuries" that the day traders do not. In response to this, there are a select group of trade execution systems that allow day traders to use what are called "hidden orders" to buy large blocks of stock without displaying it to the marketplace. (See chapter 5 for more on this topic.)

The problem is, this kind of thing will probably not change anytime soon. If you trade on the NASDAQ, this is what you will face every single day. Will it ever change? Obviously, the market makers don't want to give up their "edge." As long as this subtle form of price manipulation is allowed, Wall Street will continue to make money in these situations while the day traders are almost certain to lose it. We are to conclude but one thing about NASDAQ: that a truly "fair" market for the day trader and the investing public is a long way away.

Smoke and Mirrors in Reverse

In the last example we saw how our market maker took advantage of the day traders by "suckering" them into a position, then forcing them to close it out at a loss seconds later. The market maker manipulated the market by accumulating a large block of stock while only showing a small bid. That is not the only way the market makers can manipulate the supply and demand for their own benefit, and, in the process, cause day traders to lose money. Now we are going to see how this "smoke and mirrors" drama plays out in reverse, and how it can catch the day traders off guard. In this example the market maker will "lure" the day traders into buying stock, and then it will force them to sell it at a loss seconds later.

The Fear of Weighing Down the Market

The stock we will use in this example is Phone.com (PHCM), a NASDAQ stock that is extremely volatile. Our market maker needs to unload 5,000 shares. Because the stock is so "thin," the market maker faces the same dilemma as before: He must disguise his intentions. The market maker cannot advertise to the marketplace that he is an aggressive seller without prompting the day traders to jump ahead of him and drive the stock lower. Nor does he want to "blindside" the stock with a 5,000-share sell order, which could very easily drive it down 3 points.

Our market maker has one and only one way to sell the stock: *He must sell heavily into the strength without the day traders noticing.* How does he do this? Just like the last example, except in reverse. He will wait for a rally, then offer 100 shares for sale to the day traders. The day traders, thinking the stock is heading higher, will bombard him with buy orders. And instead of selling just 100 shares, he will sit there until his whole 5,000 piece is liquidated. The day traders will not know until it is too late that the market maker has manipulated them. Let's see how the drama plays out.

PHASE 1: THE ILLUSION OF A 100-SHARE OFFER

Our market maker (XXXX) needs to liquidate a 5,000-share position of PHCM. The strategy is to sell heavily in the next rally without the day traders noticing. How does he do that?

Phone.Com (PHCM)

Market Maker Buys			Market Maker Sells		
5	MASH	$147\frac{3}{4}$	1	XXXX	148
3	NITE	$147\frac{3}{4}$	5	ISLD	$148\frac{3}{8}$
2	SLCK	$147\frac{3}{4}$	3	RSSF	$148\frac{1}{2}$
2	COWN	$147\frac{3}{4}$	4	FLTP	$148\frac{3}{4}$

Our market maker sets the "booby" trap by offering 100 shares at 148 at the precise moment the stock appears headed higher. What the day traders don't know is that this 100-share offer is an illusion. There is far more stock for sale at 148 than the market maker is indicating.

Is Our Market Maker "Off" His Market?

One of the reasons for this kind of manipulation strategy being so successful lies in the fact that it takes advantage of the common-sense instincts of the day traders. Any day trader who is looking at the stock right now would immediately ask the question: Is the market maker selling stock at 148 "off" his market? Couldn't he sell it up, at $148\frac{3}{8}$, instead? Why is he leaving money on the table? *This is exactly what the market maker wants the day traders to think!* It is a form of reverse psychology, of bluffing.

The result? The day traders will try to take advantage of what they perceive as a weakness in the market. What they don't know is that they are walking right into a trap.

PHASE 2: THE MARKET MAKER DOES NOT BUDGE

With what they think is only 100 shares for sale at 148, the day traders are in a race to get their hands on the stock before it disappears. The day traders flood the market with buy orders. As the orders come in, our market maker "fills" every single buy order.

Phone.com (PHCM)

Market Maker Buys			Market Maker Sells		
5	MASH	$147\frac{3}{4}$	1	XXXX	148
3	NITE	$147\frac{3}{4}$	5	ISLD	$148\frac{3}{8}$
2	SLCK	$147\frac{3}{4}$	3	RSSF	$148\frac{1}{2}$
2	COWN	$147\frac{3}{4}$	4	FLTP	$148\frac{1}{4}$

Several seconds go by and the market maker is still selling heavily at 148. The day traders will start to get nervous when they see that, despite all this buying pressure, the stock is still stuck at 148. In other words, the market maker has not budged!

What you see here is a brokerage firm exploiting the system by fooling day traders into thinking there are only 100 shares for sale. Put yourself in the shoes of the day traders. Would you bombard the stock with buy orders at 148 if you saw that the seller had 5,000 shares to go at that price? No way! *This is market manipulation because the true supply and demand in the stock is intentionally hidden from view by the market maker.* There are not 100 shares for sale, there are 5,000. But you would never know it by the quoted market.

Sucker's Bet in Its Purest Form

Keep in mind that anytime the market gets manipulated, someone gets hurt. Who usually loses when a market maker hides the stock's supply and demand from view? You guessed it: the day traders. But this is capitalism, and the market maker couldn't care less who gets hurt. He accomplished his goal: He sold all of his stock at 148 before it dropped. Why should he care that the people who bought his stock from him at 148 all lost money on the trade?

When it becomes clear that XXXX is holding the stock down, the day traders will stop buying it. All of the "suckers" who just bought the stock at 148 will turn on a dime when they come to the realization that it is not going any higher until this market maker has finished selling. The buying pressure quickly subsides, and buying turns into selling.

The Market Maker Forced the Day Traders Into Paying the Spread

From the day trader's standpoint, the thing that is so frustrating about this kind of trade is not that the market maker held the stock down, or that he manipulated it. No one but the market maker has any control over that. Instead, it is the fact that the market maker's antics *forced the day traders into paying the spread*. Remember the theme from the first chapter: If you pay the spread on every trade, it will be next to impossible to make a living as a day trader. In a situation like this, once the day traders are caught off guard, fear and greed create a panic situation. When this happens it takes them "off" their game. And when they are "off" their game, they throw caution to the winds and recklessly pay the spread. In other words, they lift offers and hit bids when they should be doing the exact opposite.

Think about the psychology of this trade. In the beginning the day traders wanted to buy the stock at 148 because they thought it was going to 150, and then, when it turned against them, they wanted to sell out at 147 because they *feared* that it was headed to 145. *The day traders lost money because they bought the top and they sold the bottom.* They bought in greed, and they sold in fear. In reality, the market maker that sold stock to them at 148 and bought it back at 147 is the one that makes a nice profit at their expense.

Would the Charts, Graphs, and Research Help You Here?

It is important to drive home another of this book's major themes: Would the day trader who trades from charts, graphs, and brokerage firm recommendations have a prayer in this kind of situation? Would the price chart provide any indication to him that the market maker was manipulating the stock and preventing it from going higher? Absolutely not!

What Is Supposed to Happen Often Doesn't

The most important lesson you can learn from these kinds of situations is that things do not always go according to plan. The stock was *supposed* to trade higher than 148, but instead *it did the exact opposite. In momentum trading, what is expected does not always happen.* It is how you react to the unexpected that separates winning traders from those who consistently lose money. The problem with this situation is that it was next to impossible to tell that the market maker was "bluffing" until it was way too late. This is a sucker's bet from the start, and the day trader who is able to recognize this the fastest, and cut his losses, is the one who stays in the game over the long haul.

Backing Away from the Quoted Market

From the perspective of the day trader, one of the most unfair practices that the NASDAQ market makers engage in is something called "backing away." When it is said that a market maker is backing away from his quoted market, it means that he is not honoring a bid or an offer. In other words, the brokerage firm is trying to manipulate the market by appearing to be a seller when it is not, or is masquerading as a buyer when it has no intentions of actually buying. Why do market makers do this? For the same reason they manipulate the markets in other ways: to derail day traders and make money at their expense.

MASQUERADING AS A BUYER

The most common form of market manipulation that occurs is when a market maker "backs away" from his quoted market. In this example, our market maker (XXXX) advertises to the marketplace that he is willing to buy 2,000 shares of RMBS at 283.

Rambus (RMBS)

Market Maker Buys			Market Maker Sells		
20	XXXX	283	5	INCA	$283\frac{1}{2}$
5	NITE	$282\frac{5}{8}$	4	SHWD	284
4	PERT	$282\frac{3}{8}$	2	HRZG	$284\frac{1}{2}$
1	ISLD	282	3	ARCA	285

If the stock starts to look weak and the sell orders start coming in, our market maker will simply "back away" from his quote and not buy any stock at his advertised price.

In the eyes of the NASDAQ, "backing away" is illegal, but the market makers do it all the time. To cover his hide, our market maker may buy a token 100-share lot at 283 but will not honor the rest of his 2,000-share bid. This way, if regulators investigate, he can say he did honor his market to a certain degree because he bought 100 shares. Regardless, this is market manipulation because, even though XXXX is indicating to the market that he is a buyer of 2,000 shares at 283, he has no intention of buying that much stock. Thus, the market maker's 2,000-share bid is really nothing more than a facade, an illusion, put there for the sole purpose of confusing day traders.

Backing Away Gives the Market Makers a Huge Edge Over the Day Traders

As you know, the NASDAQ market is extremely volatile. Market conditions can change in a split second, and a stock that looks strong one minute can quickly turn weak. The reason backing away is so unfair is because it gives the market makers a huge advantage over you and me in the most volatile situations. Think about it for a moment. As day traders, are we allowed to back away from our bids and offers? If I enter a 2,000-share bid in Rambus, do I have the luxury of honoring only 100 shares if the market turns against me? Absolutely not!

Why would a market maker back away from his quoted market? Particularly in the "thinnest" and most volatile stocks, the market makers like to have the luxury of being able to "feel out the market." From their standpoint, they can "have their cake and eat it too" because they put a bid or an offer into the market, and only honor it when the market goes their way. Rest assured, if the market in Rambus quickly turned higher, our market maker certainly would not have backed away from his 2,000-share bid. Instead, if he thought he could make money on it, he would have bought all the stock he could get his hands on.

The Art of Backing Away from an Offer to Sell

We have just seen how "backing away" works when the market maker is a buyer; now let's look at an example when our market maker is a seller. The effect on the day trader can be just as devastating. This is another situation in which you must put yourself in the market maker's shoes to get a firm understanding of why he would "back away" in the first place.

Imagine that our market maker is trying to short 3,000 shares of China.com at 130 because he thinks it is headed lower. What does he do if, the split second he advertises his intentions to the marketplace to sell, the bids pile up and the stock begins to "rip" higher. Market makers do not like to get "short" at the beginning of an updraft because the stock could very easily run up 2 or 3 points in a matter of seconds. The market maker was not expecting this and it will catch him off guard. If you were the market maker, and you knew that you had just made a grave error in judgment, what is the first thing you would do? Would you sit there and blindly short 3,000 shares at 130, even though you know it is now headed higher? Why would you give your money away to the day traders?

As you know, that is the last thing you would ever want to do. The first thing you would try to do is to cancel your 3,000 short offer. The problem is that you may not be able to cancel it fast enough. Remember, there could be hundreds of day traders who are desperately trying to capitalize on your perceived mistake. And these day traders have lightning fast trade-execution systems. The only thing you can do to protect yourself from this flood of buyers is to back away from your quote. Even though you are advertising yourself to the market as a seller, you simply refuse to sell anyone any stock.

THE UPDRAFT CATCHES THE MARKET MAKER OFF GUARD

At precisely the same time that our market maker (XXXX) advertises to the marketplace that he is willing to sell 3,000 shares short at 130, the stock seems to get caught in a sudden updraft.

China.com (CHINA)

Market Maker Buys			Market Maker Sells		
10	ISLD	$129^{15}/_{16}$	30	XXXX	130
20	ARCA	$129^{15}/_{16}$	5	MASH	$130^{1}/_{4}$
9	RSSF	$129^{7}/_{8}$	8	NITE	$130^{3}/_{8}$
4	COWN	$129^{7}/_{8}$	5	JMPS	$130^{1}/_{2}$

Fearing that the stock could run up 2 or 3 points in a matter of seconds, the market maker quickly changes his mind and decides that he no longer wants to get short the stock at 130. To protect himself our market maker "backs away" from his intention to sell stock. As the day traders desperately try to lift the 3,000 shares that they see for sale at 130, they will be surprised to find out that they have been deceived. The market maker refuses to sell any more stock at that price.

Keep in mind that, in these instances of market manipulation, the same theme holds true on the sell side that does on the buy side: *The market maker will honor his sell order only if he thinks the market is going with him.* To take this example to the extreme, imagine that China.com was so volatile that it reversed its course for a second time and started heading lower again. All of those day traders who couldn't buy any stock from XXXX at 130 only three seconds ago would find out very quickly just how fast our market maker has changed his mind.

How Does the Day Trader Get Hurt?

In the back of your mind, you may be thinking, How does the day trader get hurt when the market maker backs away from his quoted market? What is the big deal if a market maker decides that he doesn't want to sell any stock at a given price? Isn't he allowed to change his mind? To answer this question, we have to ask another question: What is a market maker's main function? Why are they there in the first place? They have a responsibility, and that is to maintain an orderly market. Is the market orderly when a market maker refuses to honor his buying or selling price? Is it orderly when the investing public is deceived into thinking that a 3,000-share sell order is actually real?

We have to repeat one of this book's main themes: *When the true supply and demand in a stock gets manipulated, the day trader and the investing public are put at a severe disadvantage.* And as you know, when the day trader is put at a disadvantage, he usually loses money.

Day Traders Will Trade Against the Market Makers Only as a Last Resort

If anyone has any doubts about whether this kind of market manipulation goes on, I would suggest that you go down to any day trading firm and ask a successful momentum trader. What you will find is that, because of the things we mentioned in this chapter, day traders are so mistrustful of the market makers that they will trade against them only as a last resort. For instance, if a day trader has the option of buying stock from a market maker at 100 or buying it from another day trader on an ECN at the same price, nine out of ten times he will opt for the ECN. That is exactly why ECNs like Island (ISLD) have become so popular with day traders. When day traders trade directly with other day traders on these private trading networks, they steer clear of much of the unfair market manipulation that they encounter when trading against the market makers.

Market Manipulation Is the Exception, Not the Rule

It is also important to note that, thankfully, the kind of market manipulation we mentioned in this chapter is the exception, not the norm. It is not going to happen on every trade, and the majority of the time the NASDAQ market is orderly. However, it happens often enough to have an effect on your profit and loss if you are not careful. These antics shed some light on why so many day traders lose money when they trade NASDAQ stocks. Many times, when they lose money, it is really not their fault. They are confused by what they see. If you had to place the blame somewhere, it would be on the NASDAQ for allowing these rogue trading tactics to go on. That is why the day trader must always treat the market makers with a degree of suspicion and mistrust. *There are going to be times when the NASDAQ's quoted market cannot be trusted.* If you don't understand that now, you will learn the hard way that things are not always as they appear.

For in-depth examples of legal and illegal strategies that market makers and day traders utilize to manipulate stock prices, consult *The Day Trader's Survival Guide Video Companion.*

5

The Day Trader Strikes Back: How You and I Can Manipulate Stock Prices

The market makers on the NASDAQ are not the only ones who have the ability to manipulate stock prices. The day trader can also "bend" the rules of fair play, and sometimes it can be a very effective tool in the battle to beat the market makers at their own game. This chapter will highlight ways, legal and illegal, in which day traders manipulate stock prices.

Neutralizing the Market Maker's Edge

One of this book's major themes is that the way in which the NASDAQ system is structured gives the market makers a substantial trading advantage over the day traders and the investing public. This makes it very difficult to compete, particularly in the most volatile stocks on the NASDAQ. How can anyone be profitable under these circumstances? One of the keys to success is the ability to neutralize the edge that the market makers have. This skill can manifest itself in many different ways. It could mean the ability to make the spread as opposed to paying it, the ability to see through the smoke and mirrors and buy when the market makers are buying and sell when they are selling. And, last but not least, it could mean the ability to utilize every possible means, legal or illegal, to beat the market makers at their own game.

Manipulating the Markets Legally

As we saw in the last chapter, the market makers will "bend the rules" of fair play to take advantage of day traders. In this day and age of technology, however, the market makers are not the only ones who can stretch the rules and get away with it. The most successful day traders "fight fire with fire" and also attempt to manipulate the supply and demand in a stock to their own advantage. This is one of the ways in which profitable day traders are able to consistently beat the market makers at their own game. And many times it is not necessarily *illegal* to do so.

In the game of price manipulation, the stakes are very high. If you are able to successfully "alter" the supply and demand in a stock, it is going to give you a huge advantage over everyone else, including other day traders. Why does that give you the advantage? Because you are going to know something about the supply and demand in the stock that no one else knows, not even the market makers themselves.

Hidden Orders

One of the most prevalent ways in which day traders are able to manipulate the supply and demand in a stock *legally* is by using "hidden orders." The use of these hidden orders was a weapon that originated as the day traders' response to the questionable and unfair trading practices of the market makers. It is a tool that, in a sense, helps to level a very uneven playing field. A hidden order is an invisible bid or offer in a NASDAQ stock. It is an extremely effective weapon in the game of manipulating the supply and demand in a stock because only the day trader who has placed the order can see it. Neither the other day traders nor the market makers have any idea that it is there.

It is important to note that only the most advanced trading systems have the capability of using hidden orders. To my knowledge, the only trading systems that utilize them are those that rely upon the ECN Island (ISLD) for their executions. In addition, hidden orders are only a

NASDAQ phenomenon. They are not allowed on the New York Stock Exchange. For an up-to-date list of which trading systems use hidden orders, visit my website at *www.farrelltrading.com.*

If you asked the best of the momentum traders in the business, many would tell you that using hidden orders is an absolute necessity, and that without them it would be much more difficult to make the kind of money they now make. Why use a hidden order? To answer this, think about one of the book's earlier themes: In the most volatile stocks, the mere appearance of a large buy order can drive the stock higher.

For example, what would you do if you really wanted to buy 2,000 shares of Broadcom? What do you think will happen if you advertise that bid to the marketplace? Obviously, the other day traders will jump ahead of you. So you use a hidden order because *it allows you to bid for the stock secretly without letting anyone else know that you are trying to buy it.*

AN INVISIBLE BID THAT ONLY THE DAY TRADER SEES

One of the easiest ways in which the day trader can manipulate the supply and demand in a stock is by using a hidden order.

Broadcom (BRCM)

Market Maker Buys			Market Maker Sells		
(20	ISLD	250)	2	ARCA	251
1	ISLD	249	3	DLJP	252
1	INCA	248	1	SHWD	253
2	MLCO	247	1	NITE	254

In this example, BRCM, the day trader's 2,000-share buy order at 250 is completely invisible.

The quoted market will "hide" your buy order. In other words, it will not reflect the ISLD bid for 2,000 shares if it is hidden. Therefore all of the day traders and market makers who are watching Broadcom will be under the false impression that the market in Broadcom is 249 bid—offered at 251, and that the highest bid is at 249 for 100 shares. In reality, the highest bid in the marketplace is $1 higher at 250, and it is not for only 100 shares, it is for 2,000 shares! Thus the stock is much stronger than it appears to the market. But the only one who knows that is the day trader who placed the hidden order.

How are you able to buy the stock if the order is invisible? How can anyone else sell to you or buy from you if they don't know that you are there? The answer to this question sheds some light on why the NASDAQ is so inefficient. Remember when we said that on the NASDAQ, unlike the New York Stock Exchange, buyers and sellers can simultaneously trade stock at different prices? For instance, Merrill Lynch could be trading stock with DLJ at 247 at the same exact time that two day traders on Island are exchanging stock with each other at 252.

In our example, if someone enters a sell order on Island, their order will be routed to this hidden bid at 250. The seller will be pleasantly surprised to sell stock at 250 because it is $1 higher than what they will expect to get. Remember, all they see is a bid at 249, not 250. As long as the hidden order remains "on the books," all of the day traders using Island who try to sell "at market" will get routed to 250. In fact, ECNs like Island now have so much trading "traffic" on them that it is very easy to get a hidden order executed in the more active stocks like Yahoo!, ebay, Amazon.com, and Juniper. It is important to note that, if the hidden order is on Island, but you are trading through another ECN like Attain (ATTN) or Archipelago (ARCA), you will not get the benefit of transacting against this order. You won't see it and you won't even know that it is there. I can only speculate that in the near future, as the technology advances, this fragmentation will be eliminated.

A HIDDEN BUY ORDER IS LIKE AN INVISIBLE FISHING NET

Imagine that you wish to sell 1,000 shares of Ariba "at market." Even though the quoted market is indicating that the highest bid is at 312, anyone who sells on Island will actually get 314 for their stock because there is a hidden order there. Those not on Island will be out of luck.

The main reason for hidden orders being so deadly is that the NASDAQ allows them to be placed "through" the market. It is bad enough that they are invisible, but it is even worse when they are placed so far above or below the market that anyone watching the stock will be completely perplexed as to what is going on. This is why these kinds of orders can blindside anyone caught on the wrong side of the market. What does it mean to place an order "through" the market? *In the most volatile stocks, it means that a buy order can actually be inserted above the offer, and, conversely, a sell order can be placed below the bid.*

| 2 | DLJP | 213⅛ | 5 | COWN | 217¼ |
| 10 | GSCO | 212¼ | 4 | FBCO | 218 |

Notice that the quoted market in RMBS is 214 bid, offered at 215½. What the quoted market doesn't show is that a day trader is actually bidding for 5,000 shares $2 above the market, at 217½.

Imagine the ramifications of this if you were short the stock. At this point you would have absolutely no idea how much trouble you were in, or how much of a loss you were about to suffer. You think that the stock is trading at 215½, and it is not. In fact, it is nowhere near that price. This quoted market is misleading; it is not an accurate indication of where the buyers and sellers really are.

You Have to Be Somewhat Distrustful of the Quoted Market

Imagine that you were interested in buying 1,000 shares of a NASDAQ stock and you didn't know anything about hidden orders. If you relied upon the price quote, you would have absolutely no idea that there are buyers and sellers outside the market that you see. Remember, if a day trader wants to buy stock badly enough, he could actually place a hidden order to buy stock *dollars above* the market. The same rings true on the sell side. If that same day trader was in a panic sell situation, he could just as easily place a hidden sell order *several dollars below* the market.

If you didn't know that other day traders were doing this, you would get leveled because you would be reacting to supply and demand information that was basically wrong. This is one of the main reasons for so many people losing money trading NASDAQ stocks. In today's volatile markets these hidden orders are everywhere. In many instances they can ignite rallies and sell-offs in a stock several seconds before the marketplace actually sees it. This drives home one of this book's themes: *On the NASDAQ you have to be somewhat distrustful of the quoted market.*

At this point I'm sure you are thinking to yourself, Why would anyone ever want to buy stock *above* the market, or sell stock *below* the market? Doesn't this leave money on the table? In our last example, if stock is for sale at 215½, why would a day trader ever want to pay 217½ to *buy* it? To answer this, think of the most volatile stocks on the NASDAQ, stocks that have moved 30 points in a day, like VerticalNet, Juniper, and Ariba. These stocks can move so fast that the quote you see could literally be a fraction of a second old. In volatile times even a fraction of a second's delay could mean the difference between seeing a stock trading at 215 and at 217. This is why the most aggressive day traders cannot afford to wait until the stock moves before buying or selling, particularly if they have large positions. These stocks simply move too fast to trade them any other way.

Think back to our last example. It may seem completely absurd to pay 217½ for stock when it is for sale at 215½. But what happens if the stock is moving so fast that the stock you see for sale at 215½ is no longer there? Think what would happen if the stock was trading 4 points higher, at 221½, thirty seconds later? Was it still stupid to buy 217½ stock at that time? Absolutely not, because you would be selling it for a $4 per share profit! You will have been rewarded for being aggressive. That is why "paying through" rewards the most aggressive day traders, provided, of course, that they are lucky enough to be on the right side of the market.

Now Do You See Why You Are Dead Meat If You Use an Online Broker?

At this point it is important to emphasize another of this book's major themes: You cannot use regular online brokers to trade the most volatile NASDAQ stocks. The execution will simply be too slow to compete. Imagine that you were trying to buy 1,000 shares of RMBS through an online broker at the precise moment a hidden buy order $4 above the market was placed by another day trader? Can you imagine where your order would get executed? If a day trader with a lightning fast, high-end execution system is having trouble buying stock $4 above the market, where do you think your buy order will get filled by your online broker? That is exactly the point: You will get a horrible execution and you will probably lose money.

Using Hidden Orders as "Feelers"

If the quoted market cannot be trusted, how are the most successful day traders able to make educated guesses as to where a stock is headed? What criteria do they use to make buy and sell decisions? You may be surprised to learn that some of the very best use these hidden orders as "feelers." To shed some light on this, think of how a blind person is able to make his way across a crowded intersection. In a sense, the way a blind man approaches crossing the street is the same way that a momentum trader approaches a volatile NASDAQ stock. He uses hidden orders to "feel out" the supply and the demand in the stock much like a blind man uses his walking stick to lead him in the right direction.

"FEELING OUT" THE SUPPLY AND DEMAND WITH A HIDDEN ORDER

The day trader is putting a hidden "feeler" in at 134, ½ point higher than the bid. His strategy is simple: If he is unable to buy the stock within several seconds, he will conclude that the stock is headed higher and he will become an aggressive buyer.

PHONE.COM (PHCM)

Market Maker Buys			Market Maker Sells		
(1	ISLD	134)	3	MASH	134⅞
3	BRUT	133½	6	SLCK	135¾
5	GCSO	133	5	FBCO	136⅝
2	PIPR	132	4	SHWD	137

Why does he believe it is headed higher? If he is having trouble buying stock ½ point above the bid, where will the other market makers

---

be able to buy it? They will be forced to pay higher prices to accumulate stock. The use of a hidden order allowed the day trader to recognize this before anyone else, including the market makers themselves.

Would the Charts, Graphs, and Research Help You Here?

These examples of hidden orders help to reenforce another of this book's major themes: You cannot rely upon charts, graphs, and research in making trading decisions. Would a price chart help detect hidden orders? Would a brokerage firm recommendation give you any clue that someone is bidding $2 through the market to buy stock? No, they wouldn't. This is one of the main things that separates winning traders from those who consistently lose.

Hidden Orders Would Never Be Allowed on the NYSE

Another important point to make here is that hidden orders, like many of the other tactics of market manipulation, are strictly a NASDAQ phenomenon. This kind of thing would never be allowed on the New York Stock Exchange. Why wouldn't it be allowed? In the eyes of the New York Stock Exchange, hidden orders are not consistent with the principles of a fair and orderly market. And, in my opinion, the NYSE is absolutely right. Hidden orders are the opposite of price transparency. They don't reveal supply and demand, they hide it. This is why the use of these orders is a form of market manipulation. Remember, someone always gets hurt when someone else uses a hidden order. And most of the time it is the investing public— who don't even know that hidden orders exist.

Spoofing: An Illegal Form of Market Manipulation

"Spoofing may, with the right set of facts, constitute market manipulation because it is premised on disseminating misleading price information to the marketplace, to artificially impact the market."

—MARY SHAPIRO, CHIEF ENFORCEMENT OFFICER
National Association of Securities Dealers
The Wall Street Journal, *February 25, 2000*

Another common form of market manipulation some day traders engage in *illegally* is "spoofing." In a nutshell, spoofing is the practice of showing a large bid or offer to the market when you have no intention of actually buying or selling the stock. It is an attempt to artificially inflate or deflate a stock's price, essentially by making the stock appear stronger or weaker than it actually is. Think of it as the polar opposite of a hidden order. Remember, the goal of using a hidden order is to conceal the fact that you are trying to buy or sell stock. When you "spoof" the market, on the other hand, you are trying to mislead the marketplace into thinking that you are an aggressive buyer or seller when you are not. Why would someone try to "spoof" the market? Quite simply, *to drive it higher or lower after you have already established a position, in the hope of exiting the position at a more favorable price.*

SPOOFED!

Spoofing is a form of market manipulation because it is done to intentionally confuse the other traders watching the stock, including the market makers.

3COM (COMS)

Market Marker Buys			Market Maker Sells		
1	NITE	109	999	INCA	$109\frac{1}{16}$
5	HRZG	109	4	REDI	$109\frac{1}{8}$

5	FLTT	109	5	ISLD	109⅛
3	BEST	109	5	JPMS	109⅛

In this example of COMS on the morning of March 2, 2000, look at the size of Instinet's offer—99,900 shares, the maximum amount of stock a Level II quote can display.

Why is this spoofing? You have to ask yourself, if someone really wanted to sell 99,900 shares to the market, why would they "show" it? Whoever is showing this order has absolutely no intention of actually selling that much stock. No trader in his or her right mind would ever "show" a 99,900-share sell order to the market because they know that it would never get executed. This is an attempt by a group of day traders who are obviously short the stock to make the stock look weak, in the hope of driving it right into the ground. If they can drive the stock into the ground, they can "cover" their short positions at more favorable prices.

Ganging Up on a Stock

It is very important to mention that, most of the time, there is not a collaboration among a bunch of day traders to manipulate the market. Instead, there is a natural tendency to "gang up" on a stock once everyone is short it. Imagine that you are short the stock and you want it to trade lower. If you see someone else trying to "spoof" the market by offering 50,000 shares for sale, what difference does it make to you to add a few thousand shares yourself to his sell order to make it look even weaker? Shares at 50,000 on the offer become 52,000. Others see this and jump on behind you. Thus 52,000 becomes 62,000, etc.

Is this a safe way to trade? It actually is. Remember, the last thing you want when you are trying to "spoof" the market is for your order to get executed. You are just bluffing. And when you jump behind someone else's large sell order, it is very easy and safe to bluff because you are protected. What are the odds of someone else "lifting" 82,000 shares of stock? It would never happen in a million years! Thus there is really no risk to you in joining others in "ganging up" on the stock after you have already established a short position.

A Bunch of Bull

Whoever was trying to drive 3Com lower on the morning of March 2, 2000, quickly reversed his course.

3COM (COMS)

Market Marker Buys			Market Maker Sells		
999	INCA	109	5	ATTN	$109\frac{1}{16}$
10	MLCO	109	8	JOSE	$109\frac{1}{8}$
10	GSCO	109	4	AGIS	$109\frac{1}{8}$
10	SLCK	109	2	BTRD	$109\frac{1}{8}$

As the stock stopped falling, the 99,900-share Instinet sell order became a 99,900-share buy order!

Why the sudden change from wanting to sell 99,900 shares to now wanting to buy that much? This day trader or group of day traders on Instinet are bluffing. They are not real buyers. They are now long the stock and are trying to "goose" it higher. The second the stock trades higher, they will be right there to sell into the rally.

Spoofing Is Next to Impossible to Enforce

I must drive home the fact that spoofing, although common in the world of day trading, is illegal. I am not advocating that you use this strategy. I only mention it here to alert you to the fact that the people you are trading against might be trying to use it against you. This is why you must be prepared and expect that this kind of market manipulation will go on in the stocks you trade.

The problem with spoofing is that it is next to impossible to prevent. How can you prove that any trading violations occurred? If the day traders involved in this example were ever investigated for their antics, they would have a very easy defense. How can anyone be 100 percent sure that this is market manipulation? Yet I bet if you asked five hundred traders on Wall Street, they would all say the same thing: This 99,900-share order was a bunch of bull. This is exactly why spoofing is such a problem on the NASDAQ. It goes on all the time, but the regulators cannot do anything about it.

Does Spoofing Hurt Anyone?

As with all other forms of market manipulation, there is always someone who gets hurt when a stock is "spoofed." The fact that this time the manipulation is being done by the day traders, not the market makers, doesn't change that. Who gets hurt when someone "spoofs" the market? Anyone and everyone who is basing their buy and sell decisions on what they see. This kind of market manipulation influences buy and sell decisions because it takes advantage of the common-sense instincts of day traders. When you see a large bid, your first instinct tells you that the stock is going higher and you should buy it. And when you see a large offer, your gut will tell you to get out of your stock. *The quoted market does not lie, it is the people who are doing the quoting who do.* Spoofing is so effective because, even though most of the day traders watching the stock know that it is a bluff, *it can still move the market!*

Shorting on Downticks

The most high-profile form of illegal market manipulation in which day traders engage is shorting on downticks. As you know, when you are short the stock, you profit if it goes lower. Shorting is the opposite of going long. If you short a stock at 99, and buy it back at 98, you made the same profit as if you bought it first at 98 and sold it later at 99. Day traders love to short stocks because they usually fall much faster than they rise.

There were rules put in place many years ago that prevent traders from shorting stocks on downticks. On the NASDAQ the rules are slightly different from those on the NYSE, but the general theme is the same: *You are not allowed to short a stock once it starts falling.* In other words, you cannot sell stock short unless it is on an uptick. If you could, it would be very easy for traders to gang up on a stock and drive it right into the turf. This is what is known as a "bear raid." These "bear raids" are one of the main reasons for some NASDAQ stocks dropping 2 or 3 points in a matter of seconds. The day traders are illegally pounding the stock into the ground by shorting on downticks. How can this be done? By overselling the stock once you are long it. Let's look at an example.

INITIATING A BEAR RAID

In this example, our day trader is long 100 shares, but his intention is to "skirt" the rules of fair play and get short the stock on the way down. How does he do this? By overselling the stock: sending 100-share sell orders to every single market maker on the bid, in descending order.

EXODUS COMMUNICATIONS (EXDS)

Market Maker Buys			*Market Maker Sells*		
1	PERT	166	4	SBSH	$166\frac{7}{8}$
1	MASH	$165\frac{1}{4}$	3	MLCO	$167\frac{1}{2}$
1	GRUN	$164\frac{3}{4}$	3	MSCO	168
1	DAIN	164	4	INCA	$168\frac{7}{8}$

100-share sell order sent to PERT at 166
100-share sell order sent to MASH at $165\frac{1}{4}$
100-share sell order sent to GRUN at $164\frac{3}{4}$
100-share sell order sent to DAIN at 164

By sending sell orders to four different market makers on the way down, the day trader is quickly able to "flip" his position and go from being long 100 shares to being short 300. In addition, his selling creates downward momentum, helping to drive the stock into the ground, sending it from 166 to 164 in a matter of seconds.

Day Trading Firms Can Be Shut Down for This Practice

Unlike the other "gray" areas of market manipulation, the NASDAQ regulators are very strict in enforcing this "bear raid" rule. The stability of the markets depends on it. Perhaps you have seen the articles on this topic that have appeared in the financial papers in the last few years. Day trading firms found in violation of this rule face stiff fines, and the regulators have threatened to close firms that abuse this rule. This poses a real problem for people who run day trading firms because it is very difficult to consistently "police" your customers to make sure they are playing fair.

I must make clear that it is not my intention in this chapter or the others to point the finger at market makers or day traders. I'm simply describing the things that go on in the NASDAQ, and the environment that the day trader faces. Frankly, I don't blame any of them for using every possible means to gain an edge, even if that means bending the rules of fair play. This is a very unfair market system, and when your life's savings and your livelihood are on the line, you have to do everything you can to survive. If the NASDAQ market was truly a fair and orderly market, there would be no need for anyone to break the rules.

[6]

The Momentum Trader's Quiz: Applying What We Have Learned

The most successful momentum traders see profits because they overcome all of the obstacles that face them. We have seen firsthand the kind of antics that go on every single day on the NASDAQ: lightning-fast market movements, price manipulation, and hidden orders, to name a few. What we have is a very unfair market system that favors the Wall Street trading firms over the individual investor and the day trader. It is a very difficult world to survive in, but the people who do survive make a fortune. So how do they do it?

In this chapter we are going to apply everything we have learned so far about momentum trading. We will go step-by-step through the process of how a day trader approaches a volatile stock, and then how he is able to get his hands on it when it is in high demand and is running higher. This will give you a good indication of the mind-set and approach of the competitors you will inevitably face in the world of momentum trading.

To set the background let's use a high-percentage trading strategy: buying a strong stock on a pullback. To further aid us in this analogy, let's assume that our day trader has enough capital to buy to 1,500 shares. The stock we will use is an old favorite of momentum traders, DoubleClick.

The Strategy

The very first thing you should do is lay out your strategy. What is the plan of action on this trade? It is very simple: to buy DoubleClick on the pullback, then sell it into the rally that will inevitably follow. You must keep in mind that momentum trading is a very inexact science. There is really no way to tell when the exact time to enter the stock will be, but you must keep one theme in the back of your mind: *Do not chase the stock higher.* No matter how high the stock first goes, if you can wait until the pullback before buying, the odds of a profitable trade are much greater.

When the stock finally does pull in, wait until you see the wall of bids beginning to build up before you enter. That is as good a time as any to jump in. But it is important to note that successful momentum traders don't jump in headfirst with 1,000 shares. You should "ease" into the stock with a smaller trade size because you need to protect yourself in the event that you are wrong.

STEP 1: SNEAK INTO THE MARKET WITH A "STEALTH" BID

After watching the stock "pull back" from its highs, and determining your entry point, the very first thing you should do is to sneak into the market with a hidden bid for 500 shares.

DoubleClick (DCLK)

Market Maker Buys			Market Maker Sells		
(5	ISLD	$89^{13}/_{16}$)	6	GRUN	90
10	PIPR	$89^{3}/_{4}$	1	DLJP	$90^{3}/_{8}$
10	MLCO	$89^{3}/_{4}$	3	SHWD	$90^{5}/_{8}$
8	INCA	$89^{3}/_{4}$	8	NITE	$90^{7}/_{8}$

Once we see the wall of bids begin to build up at $89^{3}/_{4}$, that is perhaps the best time to insert our hidden buy order. It is wise to put the order in at a slightly higher price level than the buyers at $89^{3}/_{4}$, to make sure that we get "first dibs" on any stock that may come in for sale. Thus we enter a hidden buy order for 500 shares at $89^{13}/_{16}$.

This is what we mean by "feeling out" the market. In this situation, there is no middle ground. We either buy the stock at $89^{13}/_{16}$ or we don't. If we buy it, great! We should be able to sell it for a profit. If we don't buy it, *that is even better!* Why is it better to not buy the stock? Because it will prove our conviction that the stock is headed higher. Remember, the stock has pulled in, so the odds are that the next move for the stock is higher. If we don't buy the stock at $89^{13}/_{16}$ with the hidden order, that will reenforce this belief, in which case we will become aggressive buyers at slightly higher prices.

By using this hidden order, think of the trading advantage that we have over all the other market players watching the stock. That wall of buyers at $89^{3}/_{4}$ patiently waiting to buy stock have absolutely no idea that we are out-bidding them at $89^{13}/_{16}$! If we can't buy stock at $89^{13}/_{16}$, how are these market makers going to be able to buy stock at $89^{3}/_{4}$? That is just it. They are not! The wall of market makers will be forced to pay higher prices to buy stock. And the only ones who know that right now are us.

STEP 2: BECOME AN AGGRESSIVE BUYER BY LIFTING OFFERS AT HIGHER PRICES

Since we have been unable to buy our stock at $89^{13}/_{16}$, we cancel our hidden order. We are almost certain that the stock is now headed higher. These volatile stocks move so fast that we cannot afford to wait any longer. We have to get our hands on the cheapest stock that is for sale in the marketplace before anyone else does. Gruntal is a seller of 600 shares at 90. Even though that requires "paying the spread," that stock at 90 will seem very cheap in about twenty seconds, when the stock is trading up at $90^{1}/_{2}$ or higher. Without hesitation we "lift" the 600 shares that Gruntal has for sale at 90. Now the fun begins.

The next thing we want to do is make the stock appear strong. The first step in doing this is to try to draw that wall of buyers at $89^{3}/_{4}$ to a higher price. The best way to do this is to outbid them. We reenter our buy order for 500 shares, but this time at 90. And the order is not hidden. *We want the market makers and the other day traders to see it!* Remember, we have already bought 600 shares, so we don't really care if we can't buy any more stock. This is a bluff. Our goal in showing a 500-share bid at 90 to the marketplace is to force the other market makers to raise their bids.

STEP 3: FORCE THE MARKET MAKERS TO RAISE THEIR BIDS

We show our 500-share bid to the marketplace at 90 and it has an immediate effect on the stock.

DoubleClick (DCLK)

Market Maker Buys			Market Maker Sells		
5	ISLD	90	1	DLJP	$90\frac{3}{8}$
10	PIPR	90	3	SHWD	$90\frac{5}{8}$
10	MLCO	90	8	NITE	$90\frac{7}{8}$
8	INCA	90	2	MASH	$91\frac{1}{4}$

One by one, the market makers at $89\frac{3}{4}$ react by raising their bids to 90. The wall of buyers at $89\frac{3}{4}$ now becomes a wall of buyers at 90.

This has a drastic effect on the market because any day trader watching the stock will now be inclined to jump in. Others will conclude what we concluded several seconds ago: *The stock is headed higher.* Now that the day traders have been drawn into the stock, the bidding war will begin. The market makers will be forced to pay higher prices if they want to buy stock.

As the day traders bombard the stock with buy orders, we will add fuel to the fire by "spoofing" the market. When we are absolutely certain that the stock is headed higher, we cancel our bid for 500 at 90 (remember, we didn't want to buy more stock there anyway because we had already bought 600 shares) and replace it with a bid for 500 shares at 90¼.

DoubleClick (DCLK)

Market Maker Buys			Market Maker Sells		
5	ISLD	$90\frac{1}{4}$	1	DLJP	$90\frac{3}{4}$
10	PIPR	$90\frac{1}{4}$	3	SHWD	$90\frac{5}{8}$
10	MLCO	$90\frac{1}{4}$	8	NITE	$90\frac{7}{8}$
8	INCA	$90\frac{1}{4}$	2	MASH	$91\frac{1}{4}$

This is our attempt to manipulate the stock higher, and to make it appear stronger than it actually is. The buying squeeze is on.

Just as we expected, the market makers and the other day traders react to our "bluff" by lifting offers. The market makers in turn raise their bids to $90\frac{1}{4}$. In a split second the stock starts to "rip" higher, trading through $90\frac{3}{8}$, $90\frac{5}{8}$, and $90\frac{7}{8}$. As the panic buying reaches a climax, we dump our 600 shares at 91. A $600 profit (before commissions) for only a few seconds of work.

I must go on record as warning you about the dangers of spoofing the stock like we did in this example. It is extremely risky, and should only be reserved for the most seasoned of day traders. Even given that, there are only certain times when it is an advantageous strategy to use. Be forewarned: It could very easily backfire on you if you are not careful.

Success Requires That You Use Every Weapon in Your Arsenal

As you can see, the momentum trader's key to success is the ability to move quickly, and to use every weapon in his arsenal. We made a $600 profit because we did everything from using hidden orders, to manipulating the market, to selling into a buying climax. This is how your competition approaches trading a volatile stock, and you have to get into their mind-set if you are going to have any chance of success. You must keep in the back of your mind that every market movement you see could be a bluff of some kind. Yet in the end, even if day traders and market makers are trying to play games with the stock, *it is supply and demand that dictates whether a stock is going higher or lower.* If you can buy when the market needs buyers, and sell when the market needs sellers, if you can buy pullbacks and sell rallies, and avoid the damaging aspects of paying the spread, that is what will keep you in this game over the long haul.

I thought that a fitting end to our section on momentum trading would be to apply what we have learned. The goal of the quizzes in this chapter is to put you, the reader, in "the trenches." I understand that, for those of you new to day trading, many of the concepts we have talked about in this book might be foreign to your traditional way of thinking. There is no doubt that the subject matter can be difficult at times, and these quizzes will be of great help in driving home the main ideas. Before you can truly interpret and exploit the short-term movements of the market, you will need to sharpen your understanding of both the buyer's and the seller's perspective, and these quizzes will help you do that.

Momentum Trader's Quiz #1: Determining an Entry Point

Imagine that you have been actively following Exodus Communications on your NASDAQ Level II screen. Of the following two situations, which one gives you a better entry point for a long position? Note that the "inside" market is exactly the same in both examples: 101 bid, offered at 101¼.

Scenario 1:

Exodus Communications (EXDS)

Market Maker Buys			Market Maker Sells		
5	BRUT	101	10	JPMS	101¼
5	ISLD	100¾	10	PIPR	101¼
5	INCA	100½	10	FLTP	101¼
5	NITE	100	10	ATTN	101¼

Scenario 2:

Exodus Communications (EXDS)

Market Maker Buys			Market Maker Sells		
10	BRUT	101	5	JPMS	101¼
10	ISLD	101	5	PIPR	101½
10	INCA	101	5	FLTP	101¾
10	NITE	101	5	ATTN	102

Answer: Scenario 2 is a better indication of buying pressure.

Explanation: Stocks move in the path of least resistance. In one example we have a wall of buyers, and in the other we have a wall of sellers. In scenario 1 we have a wall of sellers at 101¼ and very little buying support at 101. In other words, four different traders are willing to sell stock at 101¼, while you have only one trader willing to buy stock at 101. Scenario 2 is the exact opposite. We have a wall of buyers at 101, and only one seller at 101¼. Look at how much less stock has to trade in the second example for the stock to break through 101¼—it only has to go through the 500-share lot that JP Morgan is selling. In scenario 1 even several thousand shares will not be enough buying pressure for the stock to break through 101¼ because we have 4,000 shares for sale there.

If you didn't have a Level II screen, you would never know any of this because the quoted market is the same in both examples: 101 bid, offered at 101¼. This drives home the fact that, on the NASDAQ, you need to see the depth of the market before making a buy or sell decision.

Momentum Trader's Quiz #2: Picking the Right Stock to Trade

Imagine that you are new to momentum trading and are trying to plan your strategy for the day. You are trying to decide whether to trade SUNW or CHINA when the S&P futures turn higher. Of the following two stocks, which stock is more likely to "rip" higher by several points when the overall market does begin to rally?

STOCK 1:

Sun Microsystems (SUNW)

Market Maker Buys			Market Maket Maker Sells		
10	BRUT	$95\frac{1}{8}$	10	DLJP	$95\frac{1}{4}$
10	BEST	$95\frac{1}{8}$	10	REDI	$95\frac{1}{4}$
10	HRZG	$95\frac{1}{8}$	10	OLDE	$95\frac{1}{4}$
10	MASH	$95\frac{1}{16}$	10	GRUN	$95\frac{5}{16}$

STOCK 2:

China.com (CHINA)

Market Maker Buys			Market Maker Sells		
1	SLCK	137	1	LEHM	139
1	PERT	$136\frac{1}{4}$	1	SHWD	$139\frac{7}{8}$
1	BRUT	$135\frac{3}{4}$	1	NFSC	$140\frac{3}{4}$
1	NITE	$135\frac{1}{4}$	1	COWN	$141\frac{1}{2}$

Answer: Stock 2, China.com, is much more likely to "rip" higher during a market rally.

Explanation: In a nutshell, the reason China.com is more likely to trade higher than Sun Microsystems during a market rally is that China.com is a "thin" stock while SUNW is a "thick" one. Look at the number of sellers at each price level. In SUNW, you have a wall of sellers at 95¼, followed by a second tier of stock for sale at 95⅝₆. If a buyer wanted 1,000 shares of SUNW, the stock could easily absorb the selling pressure at 95¼ and not even budge ¹⁄₁₆th of a point. In fact, DLJ would sell the whole 1,000-share piece by itself.

If that same buyer wanted to buy 1,000 shares of China.com instead, he could single-handedly drive the stock from 139 through 143, *and he still wouldn't have bought all of his stock.* The stock is so "thin" that there is no wall of sellers at any price. Here is what a 1,000-share buy order would do to China.com:

- bought 100 from LEHM at 139
- bought 100 from SHWD at 139⅞
- bought 100 from NFSC at 140¾
- bought 100 from COWN at 141½

Our buyer drove the stock from 139 to 143, and he has not finished yet. *He still has 600 shares left to buy!*

Now just imagine which of these two stocks would trade higher during a buying frenzy. What would 50,000 shares of buy orders do to these two stocks, respectively? If SunMicrosystems was able to trade higher by 1 point, China.com would probably trade higher by 5 points! Obviously, the pendulum swings both ways, and the same would be true during a market sell-off. China.com would drop a lot faster and harder than SUNW. This is exactly why day traders gravitate toward thin stocks over thick ones.

Momentum Trader's Quiz # 3: Is it a Long, or is it a Short?

Imagine that you have been trading DoubleClick (DCLK) all morning. If your Level II screen looked like it does below, which would you rather be, long or short?

DoubleClick (DCLK)					
Market Maker Buys			**Market Maker Sells**		
5	HRZG	114	20	GSCO	114¼
4	SHWD	113½	20	MLCO	114¼
5	COWN	113	20	MSCO	114¼
5	NEED	112¾	5	ISLD	114¼

Answer: Short!

Explanation: To address this situation, you have to ask yourself the following questions: Is the smart money buying or selling? Where are the "heavy hitters"—Goldman, Morgan, Merrill—and what are they doing? Is there a wall of buyers or sellers? The answer is that this stock is much more likely to head lower than higher. Why? There are two major reasons. (1) Notice that we have a wall of sellers at 114¼. (2) More important, notice *who* is doing the selling—Goldman Sachs, Morgan Stanley, and Merrill Lynch, the deepest pockets on Wall Street. *The appeareance of these major market makers as sellers can move the market by itself.* Do they know something that no one else knows? Why are they all selling together? Is it a positive for the stock that the smartest minds on Wall Street have all decided they would rather sell it than buy it? These are the kinds of questions that send day traders who are long the stock rushing to the exits.

Momentum Trader's Quiz #4: Dumping a Large Block of Stock

In this example, we are going to put you in the shoes of a major market maker. Imagine that you are the head trader at Prudential, and you have a 4,000-share position in Ariba that you have to liquidate on a day when the stock is acting strong. Which of the following two strategies will allow you to unload the stock faster, without disturbing the market?

Aggressively display the entire 4,000-share offer at 315 to the market.

Ariba (ARBA)

Market Maker Buys			Market Maker Sells		
3	DAIN	314	40	PRUS	315
4	MASH	313	3	HRZG	316
2	NITE	312	2	AGIS	317
1	RSSF	311	3	INCA	318

Manipulate the stock by displaying only 100 shares for sale at 315, and sit there until all 4,000 are sold.

Ariba (ARBA)

Market Maker Buys			Market Maker Sells		
3	DAIN	314	1	PRUS	315
4	MASH	313	3	HRZG	316
2	NITE	312	2	AGIS	317
1	RSSF	311	3	INCA	318

Answer: Situation 2

Explanation: No market makers in their right minds would ever show a 4,000-share sell to the market in a "thin" stock like Ariba, even if they actually had to sell that much stock. In this case Prudential is in a very tight predicament because they desperately need to sell 4,000 shares but cannot show it to the marketplace without driving the stock lower. Remember, in a "thin" stock the mere appearance of a large sell order by a major market maker can send the stock into free fall.

Thus the only way that Prudential can unload this 4,000-share position efficiently is by hiding their real intentions from the marketplace. The goal is to "bluff," to appear as a small seller when, in fact, they are a large one. Even though they are only displaying a sell order for 100 shares, the market maker will stay at 315 and keep selling stock until the whole 4,000-share piece is liquidated. The beauty of this strategy is that the other traders will have no way of knowing that Prudential is bluffing until it is too late. When the marketplace comes to the realization that Prudential is holding the stock down, and selling far more stock at 315 than the 100 shares they are advertising, it will be *after the fact*. At that point, from the market maker's standpoint, it won't matter because the goal will have been achieved: liquidating the entire 4,000-share position without, in the process, sending the stock into free fall.

This concludes our discussion on NASDAQ stocks. Now that we have explored the world in which momentum traders operate, I am going to take you to an entirely different planet in the day trading universe: the New York Stock Exchange. Though the risks, rewards, and trading strategies on the NYSE are very different from those on the NASDAQ, the goal is the same: to beat Wall Street at its own game.

7

The Scalp Trader and the Hunt for Razor-Thin Profits

> "No pricing mechanism is as fair and efficient as the NYSE auction where investor orders to buy and sell meet directly to trade with each other.
>
> —THE SPECIALIST ASSOCIATION

One of the most overlooked secrets of trading is that you don't need to trade the most volatile NASDAQ stocks to make a living as a day trader. Some of the best opportunities for profit are not found on the NASDAQ, but on the New York Stock Exchange instead. Why do some people say that the NYSE is an easier market to trade? Is it true that if more people traded NYSE stocks than NASDAQ stocks, the failure rate among day traders would be lower? This chapter will answer those questions.

Is the NYSE an Easier Market to Trade?

Of all the different types of day traders who have emerged in the last few years, the scalp trader is by far the most misunderstood. There seems to be a prevailing stereotype in today's marketplace that the only legitimate way to make a living as a day trader is to trade the most volatile NASDAQ stocks. I hope that the next few chapters will help to change that opinion. The problem is, scalp traders are considered "out of the mainstream," so they don't get the attention that their momentum trading counterparts do. How many day trading firms do you know that steer their clients away from NASDAQ and toward NYSE stocks? How many day traders do you ever read about in the newspapers who made their fortunes trading New York Stock Exchange stocks? It is a very rare occurrence when the scalp trader gets that kind of attention in the media.

When I tell people that I make my living trading primarily New York Stock Exchange stocks, not NASDAQ stocks, I usually get two reactions: surprise and confusion. The questions asked are always the same: *How can you possibly make a living trading NYSE stocks? How can you make any money in stocks that really don't move? Wouldn't you rather be where the action is, on the NASDAQ?* Part of the reason for this reaction is that scalpers are not the superstar traders you read about in newspapers. Scalp traders are not the ones making $100,000 in a single afternoon, or the ones making seven-figure salaries at the age of twenty-five. However, they are also not the ones losing their life's savings in a single month.

Scalp Traders Cannot Expect to Make the "Big Bucks" That Momentum Traders Do

The fact of the matter is that the scalp trader cannot expect to make the kind of money that successful momentum traders make. The only way you could make that kind of money would be to trade the most volatile stocks in the marketplace, and the NYSE stocks that the scalp trader gravitates toward are not in that category. Quite simply, the scalp trader's universe is not capable of producing the wide price swings that you see in momentum stocks. In fact, if they were, scalpers would probably avoid them because they would simply be too volatile. Remember, when you are taking down 4,000 shares at a time, even an ⅛th-point move can be significant.

So what is the catch? Why steer clear of the NASDAQ and trade a market segment that is much less exciting, and potentially less profitable? *Because there are certain times when the New York Stock Exchange is an easier market to trade.* The profits may not be as big, but the odds of making them are better. And in many of these trades you can actually get away with using a regular online broker instead of having to rely upon a higher-cost, direct-access system. The reason for this is that, in a sense, the NYSE is a more level playing field than the NASDAQ, and that greatly increases the chances of being consistently profitable.

At this point we need to redefine what it means to be a scalp trader. Unlike the momentum trader, the scalp trader is not looking for big moves in volatile stocks. Instead, he is looking for small moves in less volatile stocks. The scalp trader's world is one of $\frac{1}{16}$ths, $\frac{1}{8}$ths, and $\frac{1}{4}$s. It could literally mean buying the same stock four separate times at 7, and selling it at $7\frac{1}{16}$, throughout the trading day. How can the scalp trader make a living on profits so "razor" thin? Because he or she trades "size": 2,000- , 3,000- , 4,000-share lots. *You cannot make a decent living on $\frac{1}{16}$ths and $\frac{1}{8}$ths if you trade anything less than 2,000-share lots.*

Why Is the NYSE a More Level Playing Field Than the NASDAQ?

There are several basic reasons for the NYSE being an easier market to trade than the NASDAQ. Generally speaking, the specialist has less of a trading edge over the day trader on the New York Stock Exchange than the market makers enjoy on NASDAQ. In other words, the specialist system on the NYSE is a fairer system for the investing public than the NASDAQ's market-maker system. And that "fairness" spills over into the day trader's world, and gives him a greater chance of being profitable.

> "Our desire to bring supply and demand into balance is what sets us apart."
>
> —WILLIAM JOHNSTON, PRESIDENT
> *New York Stock Exchange*
> The New York Times, *October 21, 1999*

The foundation of any efficient and fair marketplace is its ability to bring supply and demand into balance at all times. This is what sets the NYSE apart from the NASDAQ. The specialist system ensures that both buyers and sellers always get the best possible price, no matter what the market conditions may be. The buyer buys the cheapest stock available for sale in the marketplace, and the seller always sells stock to the buyer willing to pay the highest price.

Unlike the NASDAQ, the NYSE's Quoted Market Can Be Trusted

One of the main components for the NYSE sometimes being an easier market to trade is because the quoted market is actually *real*. In other words, the price quote is an accurate reflection of the true supply and demand in the stock. When you pull up a quote, what you see is what you get. Unlike the NASDAQ, you can actually trust the bid and the ask prices that you see. You can trust them because you are not going to have stock changing hands $1 below or $1 above the bid or the ask prices like you do on the NASDAQ. For example, when you see a stock that is bid for 100 shares at 6, it is illegal for the stock to trade 100 shares at 5¾ until the buyer at 6 is filled. As you now know, that is not the case on the NASDAQ, where it is not uncommon for stocks to trade all over the map, above and below the quoted market.

It seems like common sense that all financial markets would operate under this premise. Without question, 90 percent of the time they do. But it is during that other 10 percent of the time, usually under extremely volatile and fast-moving circumstances, that the "cracks" in the system are brought to light. As a day trader, it is during these extreme situations that you will witness firsthand why the New York Stock Exchange's specialist system keeps a fairer and more orderly market than the NASDAQ's market-maker system.

THE REAL MARKET

The foundation behind the specialist system on the NYSE being so fair and orderly is the fact that the quoted market is "real." Even under the most volatile conditions, stock prices cannot trade outside the parameters of the quoted market, below the bid or above the ask.

| GM | $71-71\frac{1}{4}$ | $1,000 \times 1,000$ |

For instance, if I am willing to buy 1,000 shares of General Motors at 71, it is illegal for 1,000 shares to trade below 71 at the specialist's post without my buy order being executed first.

The NASDAQ Is a Fragmented Market

This is one of the main areas in which the NYSE and the NASDAQ differ. While the specialist's market keeps the buyers and sellers "in check," many times the NASDAQ market makers do not. The problem is, there are so many market makers buying and selling stock at the same time that the NASDAQ market becomes fragmented. As we discussed in earlier chapters, market makers on NASDAQ could be simultaneously trading stock at different price levels. For instance, Morgan Stanley and Goldman Sachs could be trading stock at 71 while Island and DLJ are trading stock at 73. Remember our earlier example in MP3, the initial public offering that was trading at 92 and 104 *at the same time?* That is why the quoted market on the NASDAQ can sometimes be a "phantom market" because, during volatile times, the bid and the ask are not accurate reflections of where stock is actually changing hands. This is not true of the NYSE.

It is important to note that this inefficiency is not intentional. It is a by-product of a system that does not have a centralized place where all buy and sell orders are kept. That is perhaps the biggest difference between the New York Stock Exchange and the NASDAQ. The specialist controls all of the traffic on the NYSE, while on NASDAQ the traffic is split among different trading networks.

In addition to that, as we have mentioned before, there are different order-handling rules on the two exchanges, and without question the NYSE's order-handling rules are fairer to the trading public. Think back to chapter 2 and our limit-order experiment between the NASDAQ stocks (MCICP) and the NYSE stock (EDL). As you know, our limit order on the NYSE stock was immediately reflected in the market, yet our limit order on NASDAQ never was. This is one of the reasons for the NYSE being an easier market to trade. Thus it can be said that the fairness of the NYSE essentially reduces the trading edge that the specialist has over the day trader, and this is what gives the scalp trader a realistic chance for profit.

The basic premise behind why the specialist system is so fair is that the specialist is obligated to give priority to a customer order over his own. In other words, if the specialist wants to buy stock at 10, and a day trader comes along who also wants to buy stock at 10, the specialist must let the day trader step in front of him. Exploiting this rule allows day traders to, essentially, extract profits from the stock that would normally be reserved for the specialist. In other words, the rule allows the day trader to take food out of the specialist's mouth.

In addition, the scalp trader is also not going to encounter the level of market manipulation that the momentum trader has to deal with on the NASDAQ. The specialist will, on occasion, try certain tactics in an attempt to derail scalp traders (see chapter 9), but this is not nearly as widespread on the NYSE as it is on the NASDAQ. All of those unfair NASDAQ market antics that we described in earlier chapters, including hidden orders, are simply not allowed to occur on the New York Stock Exchange. In fact, the very presence of the NYSE's centralized order-handling system prevents just about every form of market manipulation that we have studied (with the exception of spoofing). Remember, any trading violations in an NYSE stock fall directly on the specialist's lap.

> **"No other market structure has such a pivotal figure held responsible and answerable for its orderly operation."**
>
> **—THE SPECIALIST ASSOCIATION**

Trading Higher-Priced NYSE Stocks

Generally speaking, the scalp trader should avoid the most volatile New York Stock Exchange stocks. The problem with these stocks is that the higher-priced and more volatile the stock, the greater the edge that the specialist has over the day trader. However, there are going to be a few times when the playing field in these big-name stocks is "safe" to trade, and I want to mention one such example here. The one time when it is "safe" enough for the scalp trader to venture from the safe harbor of the lower-priced stocks and toward the high-flying ones is when one of these Dow stocks encounters an extreme sell imbalance on the open.

Playing the Specialist's Game

There is an old saying in trading: To be successful, you have to be greedy when everyone else is fearful, and fearful when everyone else is greedy. There is no better example of putting this saying to work than by buying NYSE–listed large-cap stocks during a period of bad news. What are these large-cap stocks? The market-leading names you see in the news every single day: the Dow stocks, including Disney, McDonald's, and Hewlett Packard.

Did you ever wonder how the best scalp traders on Wall Street play a blue-chip stock like Procter & Gamble, IBM, or Computer Associates on a day when the stock opens down 20 or 30 points? Did you know that, when these stocks open on bad news, the opening "print" many times is the lowest the stock will trade for the entire day? Scalp traders who trade the New York Stock Exchange stocks know a secret that the investing public is unaware of: that one of the highest-percentage trades of the day is buying with the specialist on bad news.

The Role of the Specialist Revisited

To understand what makes this trade so successful, you have to understand the nature of the New York Stock Exchange. This will serve as a good "refresher course" for what we talked about in earlier chapters. As you know, the specialist keeps the market fair and orderly by risking his own capital. This ensures that the trading in the stock remains smooth because the specialist steps in to buy stock when there are no buyers, and sells stock when there are no sellers. If 100,000 shares need to be sold and there are no buyers, the specialist will buy the stock himself. And if 100,000 need to be bought and there are no sellers, the specialist will sell it from his own account. Thus it can be said that the specialist is truly the buyer and the seller of last resort.

> "Specialists bring buyers and sellers together, enabling a transaction to take place that otherwise would not have occurred."
>
> —THE SPECIALIST ASSOCIATION

The Specialist Is in the Business of Trading Against His Customers

Why would the specialist risk his or her own capital? Why would he put millions of dollars on the line every single day? The specialist risks money to make money. How does he make money? On the profit made by taking the other side of your trade. The specialist is essentially in the business of trading against the investing public. Every profit he makes comes at your, my, and the investing public's expense. He can make millions of dollars over the course of the year by doing this.

The Specialist Has a License to Print Money

It has often been said that, because he is in the business of trading against his customers, the specialist has a "license to print money." Essentially, the specialist trades off privileged supply and demand information that the rest of the investing community does not have. Are there large institutional buyers interested in buying stock? Who has been selling the stock heavily all morning? These are all questions that only the specialist knows the answers to. And having this information is exactly why he is able to consistently make money, week in and week out, in the trading in his particular stock.

So does the specialist really have a license to print money? During extreme buy and sell imbalances, you may be surprised to know that *he actually does.* And this is where the day trader can exploit the specialist system, and make money the same way the specialist does.

The Procter & Gamble Trade

To understand how this trade works, you must put yourself in the specialist's shoes and examine his actions during an extreme sell imbalance. There is no better example of this than Procter & Gamble on the morning of March 7, 2000. On that morning, Procter & Gamble issued an earnings warning. By 8:30 A.M. every major brokerage firm on Wall Street had downgraded the stock.

In this case the news was so bad that the stock was inundated with sell orders in the minutes before the market opened. Remember, the specialist must be the buyer of last resort when no other buyers can be found. What do you do if the news is so bad that by 9:30 A.M. you have over 7 million shares of sell orders on your books, but you can't find enough buyers to match them? This is exactly the dilemma that the specialist faced. Remember, every buyer has a seller, and you cannot open the stock for trading until all of those market sell orders are matched with buyers.

The Specialist Stepped Up to the Plate

Thus if the sell orders on your books cannot be "matched" with buyers, you will be forced to "step up to the plate," risk your own trading capital, and buy the stock, even if that means buying 1 million shares! What the investing public doesn't understand about this situation is that the specialist can make a fortune from these extreme situations by exploiting the investing public's sense of fear. The news is so bad that the investing public wants out, at any price. And who is there to buy the stock from them? The specialist. The secret is that the specialist is allowed by the rules of the exchange *to name his own price,* provided it is "fair and orderly." If you were forced into buying 1 million shares of PG, but you could name your price, no matter how low, what price would you name? Would it be high, or would it be low, and in whose best interests would the price you set be? Yours or the sellers'?

The Specialist Will Intentionally Overshoot the Market

This is why, when markets open on bad news, the low trade of the day is often the "opening print." The specialist will intentionally overshoot the market in the hope of profiting at the expense of the investing public. He will open the stock abnormally low, buy all of the stock from the investing public, and then immediately take it higher. This is exactly what happened in Procter & Gamble. When the public is dumping shares in panic and fear, the specialist is greedily buying all of the stock from them at discounted prices. In these extreme sell imbalances, the specialist knows something that the investing public does not: When the investing public all rush for the exits at the same time, they become their own worst enemy. This is exactly what creates a market bottom. After the public has finished selling, the stock has nowhere to go but up.

Over 7 Million Shares Traded on the Opening Print

In the case of Procter & Gamble, it took the specialist until 10:12 EST to finally open the stock for trading, and he opened it down 29$\frac{7}{16}$, at 58. Over 7 million shares changed hands on the opening print, and undoubtedly the specialist was a huge buyer of this now "cheap" stock. In fact, the only reason he opened the stock at 58 in the first place was because that was a low enough price level to make sure that he wouldn't lose money on his rather substantial long position. Remember, the specialist is the best trader in the world in his particular stock and has more information on the supply and demand in the stock than anyone else. You have to ask yourself the following question: Would he have bought 1 million shares for himself, and picked 58 as an opening price, because he thought the stock would trade *lower* than that? Absolutely not.

After Opening the Stock Low, the Specialist Guided It Higher

What happened next is a great example of the trading edge that the specialist has over the investing public. What would be the first thing you would try to do after buying a huge position at 58? You would try to guide the stock higher! And that is exactly what the specialist did. By 10:13, a full minute after the stock opened for trading at 58, it was trading ½ a point higher, at 58½. By 10:28, the stock was at 60, and by 10:43, the stock was at 62. It is not coincidence that it happened this way. The specialist knew exactly what he was doing. Think of how much the specialist stands to profit by buying stock at 58 on the open, and selling it on the way up at 60, 61, and 62 in the minutes that followed. Hundreds of thousands, or even millions of dollars, if the position was large enough.

Riding the Specialist's Back

So how can the day trader profit from a sell imbalance like this? Quite simply, the way the day trader can make money on this situation is "by riding the specialist's back." In other words, buying stock with the specialist on the opening print, and selling it into the updraft that should follow. If the day trader had done that here, he would have bought stock at 58, and sold it minutes later for a nice profit at 60, 61, or 62.

The logic behind this approach is very simple: As you know, the NYSE rules dictate that customer orders must be filled before the specialist's. For example, if both you and the specialist are on the bid at the same price, the specialist must fill your order before he fills his own. Market buy orders on the open get executed at the opening price. So a buy at market will get executed at the exact price the specialist pays to buy the block of stock on the open.

This example sheds light on one of the major premises of day trading NYSE–listed stocks. Any day trader who trades New York Stock Exchange stocks must trade "with" the specialist, not against him. He must buy when the specialist buys, and sell when the specialist sells. This is the day trader's equivalent of betting with the house, of being on the dealer's side of the blackjack table at a Las Vegas casino. If the day trader does this consistently, over time the odds are that he will make very good money. Why are the odds on his making money? Because he is mirroring the actions of the best trader in the world in that particular stock, the specialist. If he does not, and he trades against the specialist, over time the specialist will inevitably end up making money at the day trader's expense. On the NYSE, this is one of the foundations behind what separates winning day traders from those who consistently lose money.

We will now switch gears and focus exclusively on the universe of lower-priced issues. Even within the New York Stock Exchange universe, some stocks are easier to trade than others. The general rule of thumb that the scalp trader follows is that the *higher priced the NYSE stock is, the harder it is to trade profitably.* In other words, from the scalp trader's perspective it is easier to trade a $10 stock profitably than it is to trade a $100 stock. The example we just described, Procter & Gamble, is the exception, not the rule. From my own experience, I would much rather trade a 3,000-share lot of Western Digital (WDC) at $7, or Rite Aid at $6, than a 300-share lot of Seagate (SEG) at $70 or Merrill Lynch (MER) at $100.

There Is More "Juice" in the Lower-Priced Stocks

What the investing public doesn't understand about scalp trading on the New York Stock Exchange is that it is typically easier to make $250 on 4,000 shares of a $4 stock than it is to attempt to make $250 on 400 shares of a $40 stock. The $4 stock only has to go $\frac{1}{16}$th of a point to be "in the money," whereas the $40 stock has to go $\frac{5}{8}$th of a point, even though in both examples, only $16,000 of trading capital is at risk. It is far easier to make a 1/16th-point profit than it is to make a 5/8th-point profit, regardless of the amount of stock you are trading.

Stock Price	Number of Shares Needed to Make $250	Trading Capital at Risk
$4	4,000	$16,000 + 1/16th point
$40	400	$16,000 + 5/8th point

The rule of thumb that the scalp trader follows is that (1) the higher priced the stock, the greater the trading advantage the specialist has, and (2) the more volatile the stock, the greater the trading advantage the specialist has. This is another way of saying that the slower moving and lower priced the stock is, the greater the chance that the scalp trader will make a profit. And, as you know, this is in contrast to the momentum trader on the NASDAQ, who usually gravitates toward higher-priced stocks.

In the Game of Sixteenths and Eighths, Making the Spread Is the Key to Profitability

Now that we have touched briefly on the mind-set of a successful scalp trader, it is time to focus exclusively on the domain of lower-priced stocks. We have to reiterate one of the themes that this book drives home: You must always look to use the bid-ask spread to your advantage. *If you pay the spread on every trade, it will be next to impossible to make a living as a scalp trader.* In this game of razor-thin profit margins of 1/16ths and 1/8ths, the ability to make the spread could be the difference between a winning and a losing trade.

The Scalp Trader Is Rewarded for Trading "Size"

By using a regular online broker to trade New York Stock Exchange stocks, the scalp trader is rewarded for trading large blocks of stock at a time. And he is penalized for trading smaller lots. This is because he pays the same commission for a 100-share trade as he does for a 5,000-share trade

Trade Size	Profit on $\frac{1}{16}$th	Net Profit After $20 Round-Trip Commission
100	$6.25	−$13.75
1,000	$62.50	+$42.50
2,000	$125.00	+$105.00
3,000	$187.50	+$167.50
4,000	$250.00	+$230.00

These fixed-rate commissions allow the scalp trader to make a living on $\frac{1}{16}$th- and $\frac{1}{8}$th-point profits, provided of course that he trades large blocks of stock. If he doesn't trade "size," he will not be able to make a living on razor-thin profits. Instead, to be profitable on smaller blocks of stock, he will be forced into holding out for larger moves.

On the NYSE, the Odds Favor the Lower-Priced Stocks

One of the main reasons for the scalp trader generally shying away from the higher-priced stocks and gravitating toward stocks in the $5 to $10 range is because of the bid-ask spread. This is a great situation, because a $\frac{1}{16}$th-point spread on 1,000 shares of a $5 stock is like making a $\frac{5}{8}$-point spread on 100 shares of a $50 stock! In other words, even though you are risking the same amount of capital, the odds are better on the lower-priced stock. It is very difficult to make a ⅝-point profit by exploiting the bid–ask spread, yet it is very easy to make a quick ¹⁄₁₆th-point spread. This is what we mean when we say that a ¹⁄₁₆th-point profit on 2,000 shares is easier to come by than a ⅝th-point profit on 200 shares. I hope I have made my point clear. This universe of lower-priced NYSE stocks provides some of the best odds on Wall Street for outsiders like you and me to be consistently profitable.

The first question we have to ask is why lower-priced stocks are easier to trade. Why is the specialist's edge less in a $6 stock than it is in a $60 stock? Why would the scalper rather attempt to make ¹⁄₁₆th on 3,000 shares of a $6 stock than ½ point on 300 shares of a $60 stock? The answer is that, from a scalp trader's perspective, supply and demand imbalances are much easier to read on a $10 stock than they are on a $100 stock. Why are they easier to read? *Because price movement in lower-priced stocks is completely dictated by changes in the bid size and the ask size, and that is not true of higher-priced stocks.* This is exactly what gives the scalp trader a fighting chance in these lower-priced stocks.

To understand how this works, let's review a few major principles from earlier in this book. Remember when we said in the first chapter that the momentum trader and the scalp trader read the supply and demand information differently? Momentum traders typically look for a wall of buyers or a wall of sellers to help them predict if the next move in the stock is higher or lower. But remember, NYSE traders do not have the luxury of seeing market depth like you can on a NASDAQ Level II screen. Keep in mind that only the specialist knows the depth of the market on the New York Stock Exchange.

So if the scalp trader can't read the depth of the market like a momentum trader can on the NASDAQ, what does he use to make a buy or a sell decision? To answer this, let's look at an example in Western Digital, which at the time I'm writing this is trading at $7 per share.

Extracting a $\frac{1}{16}$-Point Profit with the "Lift and Place"

There are many different ways to approach the game of making razor-thin profits. The reality is that there is no one method that is consistently better than the others when it comes to trading NYSE stocks. The best scalp traders are the ones who know when to use certain strategies and when not to, and to last in this game, you need to have a certain degree of creativity. We will now discuss one of the ways in which the scalp trader is able to extract a $\frac{1}{16}$th-point profit on a large block of stock on the New York Stock Exchange. The strategy is something I call the "lift and place." There is an allure to this kind of trade because, if it goes your way, you can make a $300 profit in about five or ten seconds.

Basically, the "lift and place" is a strategy of exploiting a temporary supply and demand imbalance in a lower-priced stock. It relies upon quick instincts because the imbalance may only last for several seconds before it is rectified and the opportunity for profit has passed. In a nutshell, the $\frac{1}{16}$-point profit that the scalp trader makes is made directly at the expense of the large institutional buyers in the stock.

Parameters for the "Lift and Place"

Goal: *To extract a $\frac{1}{16}$-point profit on a temporary supply/demand imbalance*

Types of Stock: *NYSE stocks below $10 on days when volume is high and buying interest is strong*

Kinds of Stocks: *Widely held stocks, including Western Digital (WDC), Rite Aid (RAD), HealthSouth (HRC), Kmart (KM), Silicon Graphics (SGI), Office Depot (ODP)*

Warning: *Avoid any stock if it is trading below 1 million shares or is down on the day*

Trade Size: *Between 2,000- and 5,000-share lots*

Order Type: *Limit orders only*

Strategy for the Buy: *Wait for institutional buyers to take large chunks out of the ask size and then "lift" the last remaining stock at that price level*

Strategy for the Sell: *Immediately place the stock up for sale $\frac{1}{16}$th point higher*

Let's look at a quick example of how the "lift and place" works, and then we will go into an explanation of why the trading strategy is successful. Assume that you have been watching Kmart on a day when the trading volume is high. You pull up your real-time quote and it reads:

KM $9–9\frac{1}{16}$ **350,000 × 350,000**

The quote is telling us that there are 350,000 shares willing to be bought at 9 and 350,000 shares willing to be sold at $9\frac{1}{16}$. Supply and demand are in perfect balance, and there is no opportunity for profit. This means that, right now, there is no reason for the scalp trader to get involved. He must sit on his hands and wait until this supply and demand balance becomes an *imbalance.* Then, and only then, will the opportunity for a quick profit arise.

Imagine that, as we are watching the stock, we notice a spurt of trading activity occurring at $9\frac{1}{16}$. The ask size changes: 350,000 becomes 300,000 . . . 300,000 becomes 250,000 . . . 250,000 becomes 200,000 . . . right down to 100,000. In other words, the 350,000 shares for sale at $9\frac{1}{16}$ are disappearing in 50,000- and 100,000–share clips!

KM   **$9-9\frac{1}{16}$**   **350,000 × 100,000**

Now notice the changes in the parameters of the market. Remember when there were 350,000 shares for sale at $9\frac{1}{16}$? Now there are only 100,000 shares left. From the scalp trader's perspective, the market is starting to become lopsided. This is the first indication of a supply and demand imbalance.

The buying at $9\frac{1}{16}$ continues until the market becomes completely out of balance. Look at the ask size now: only 5,000 shares left.

KM   **$9-9\frac{1}{16}$**   **350,000 × 5,000**

In a matter of seconds, Kmart went from having an ask size of 350,000 to one of 5,000. In other words, 345,000 shares have been lifted at $9\frac{1}{16}$. The market is now truly lopsided. This is the opportunity that the scalp trader has been waiting for.

The market is indicating that the stock is headed higher. There are 350,000 shares willing to be bought at 9, but only 5,000 shares willing to be sold at $9\frac{1}{16}$. Something has to give. Without hesitation, the scalp trader buys the remaining 5,000 shares. The first phase of the lift and place has been accomplished. The scalp trader has grabbed the last block of cheap stock at $9\frac{1}{16}$. There is no longer any stock for sale at $9\frac{1}{16}$.

KM   **$9-9\frac{1}{8}$**   **350,000 × 20,000**

Once the scalp trader has bought the last remaining 5,000 shares for sale at $9\frac{1}{16}$, he cannot waste any more time. He must immediately put the stock up for sale $\frac{1}{16}$th of a point higher than where it was bought, at $9\frac{1}{8}$. He must get in line behind the sellers there before him, and to do this, *he must use a limit order.* Notice the ask size now. There are already 20,000 shares for sale at 9⅛. He is also a seller of stock at 9⅛, so he must get in line behind those 20,000 shares, bringing the ask size to 25,000.

| KM | 9–9⅛ | 350,000 × 25,000 |

When the specialist receives the scalp trader's sell order for 5,000 shares on a 9⅛ limit, he adds it to the 20,000 shares that are already for sale at 9⅛. Thus the ask size changes from 20,000 to 25,000.

A very important event is occurring. The buyers at 9 have become impatient, and are raising their bids to 9¹⁄₁₆. As the bid size at 9¹⁄₁₆ becomes larger, it creates a wall of buying support, and that makes it more likely that the scalp trader's stock at 9⅛ will trade.

| KM | 9¹⁄₁₆–9⅛ | 350,000 × 25,000 |

The same factor that caused all of the stock at 9¹⁄₁₆ to be lifted minutes earlier now causes a spurt of buying at 9⅛. In other words, the buying momentum at 9¹⁄₁₆ has finally spilled over to 9⅛. The result? The 25,000 shares for sale at 9⅛ get lifted in a matter of seconds, including the scalp trader's 5,000.

| KM | 9¹⁄₁₆–9³⁄₁₆ | 350,000 × 20,000 |

Notice that all of the 9⅛ stock that was for sale has been cleaned out. The scalp trader bought 5,000 shares at 9¹⁄₁₆, and sold it at 9⅛. He made ¹⁄₁₆th point, or $312.50 (before commission). In an ideal situation, that is how the "lift and place" works.

As you can see, the "lift and place," in its simplest form, is a bet that the momentum created by the institutional buyers will spill over into the next highest price level. To understand why this trade is successful, you need to touch upon the mechanics of how a large mutual fund buys stock. When the scalp trader is interested in buying a lower-priced NYSE stock, he is usually looking to buy 2,000 to 5,000 shares. But when a mutual fund is interested in buying one of these "cheaper" stocks, it may be interested in buying *several million shares* at a time. Think about it. If you are a mutual fund like Fidelity or Investco, with billions of dollars of trading capital that you must put to work in the market, how do you approach buying a $9 stock like Kmart? Are you going to waste your time with a 50,000- or 100,000-share position? Absolutely not. Even if you bought 1 million shares, on paper that is only a $9-million position. If you were managing $2 billion, that wouldn't even put a dent in the portfolio.

My point here is that these institutions have huge appetites. When they enter the market to buy stock, they don't waste time. They buy it in "size." It is not uncommon for them to take down 50,000 or 100,000 shares in a single clip. If you watch a stock like Kmart, you will see huge block "prints" of 20,000, 50,000, or 100,000 shares going across the tape all day long. These lower-priced stocks are extremely liquid, and on a good day will trade 5 million shares or more. With this much volume, you need to let the institutions do the dirty work for you. Once you have established a position, let the deep pockets take the stock higher. Without them, the stock goes nowhere.

FOLLOW THE TRAIL OF THE INSTITUTIONAL "PRINTS"

How do you know that the institutions are buying? Because you see the ask size getting "eaten away" in large chunks.

HRC	$5-5\frac{1}{16}$	$400,000 \times 400,000$

In this example, when you see the ask size in HealthSouth (HRC) quickly go from 400,000 shares to 40,000 shares, that is a clear sign that the "deep pockets" are buying the stock.

HRC	$5-5\frac{1}{16}$	$400,000 \times 40,000$

In the back of your mind, you have to believe that, if the institutions are willing to buy massive blocks of stock at $5\frac{1}{16}$, they will probably also pay $5\frac{1}{8}$ once all of the stock at $5\frac{1}{16}$ is gone. What is $\frac{1}{16}$th of a point to a $4-billion mutual fund that needs to accumulate 1 million shares of HealthSouth? If the scalp trader only employs the "lift and place" when the institutions are active, the odds of making the $\frac{1}{16}$th-point profit go up substantially.

A Real-Life Example of the "Lift and Place"

I want to show you a real-life example of the "lift and place," which I was involved in on March 16, 2000. This is a textbook example of the mechanics behind the trade when everything goes according to plan. The stock I was trading was Rite Aid. I was initially attracted to the stock on March 16 because it was trading high volume. By 2 P.M., the stock had traded almost 7 million shares, and was up ¼ point on the day. Keep in mind that, for a $6 stock like Rite Aid, even a ¼-point move on heavy volume is significant.

Two Block Trades Caught My Attention

At 2 P.M. I pulled up my real-time quote and it read as follows:

2:00	RAD	$5^{13}/_{16}$–$5^{7}/_8$	28,200 × 59,600

What caught my attention initially were two block trades that occurred right in sync: 10,000 shares at $5^{7}/_8$, followed by 20,000 shares at $5^{7}/_8$. Immediately after these two large block trades, the quote changed to:

| **2:00** | **RAD** | $5^{13}/_{16}$–$5^{7}/_{8}$ | $28,000 \times 23,000$ |

The first rule of the "lift and place" trade was validated: strong evidence of institutional buyers eating large chunks out of the ask size. The buying at $5^{7}/_{8}$ continued for several more seconds, until the quote read:

| **2:00** | **RAD** | $5^{13}/_{16}$–$5^{7}/_{8}$ | $29,200 \times 10,500$ |

In the thirty seconds that I had been watching the stock, over 49,000 shares had traded at $5^{7}/_{8}$! This was enough evidence for me, and I took action. I entered a buy for 5,000 shares on a $5^{7}/_{8}$ limit. I immediately got my fill report, and another wave of buyers followed me. About two seconds later, the entire 10,500-share piece remaining for sale at $5^{7}/_{8}$ was cleaned out. I wasted absolutely no time in putting the stock up for sale. In fact, I entered the sell at $5^{15}/_{16}$ about one second after I got the fill report back on my buy of 5,000 shares. It is so important to get the sell order in quickly because you do not know how long the buying momentum will last.

| **2:01** | **RAD** | $5^{13}/_{16}$–$5^{7}/_{8}$ | $29,200 \times 10,500$ |

became

| **2:01** | **RAD** | $5^{13}/_{16}$–$5^{15}/_{16}$ | $29,100 \times 11,000$ |

The Bids Began to Build Up

Once all of the $5^{7}/_{8}$ stock was lifted, the buyers at $5^{13}/_{16}$ became impatient. Just as I had suspected, they began raising their bids to $5^{7}/_{8}$. The 29,000-share bid at $5^{13}/_{16}$ that we saw at 2 P.M. moved up to $5^{7}/_{8}$ at 2:01P.M. This is always a good sign because this is that wall of buying support that we talked about. The bigger the wall at $5^{7}/_{8}$, the greater the likelihood that our sell order at $5^{15}/_{16}$ will trade quickly.

| **2:01** | **RAD** | $5^{13}/_{16}$–$5^{15}/_{16}$ | $29,100 \times 11,000$ |

became

| **2:01** | **RAD** | $5^{7}/_{8}$–$5^{15}/_{16}$ | $29,000 \times 11,000$ |

Once I had "gotten in line" with my sell order at $5^{15}/_{16}$, I had to wait. By 2:04, I had sold my stock.

| 2:04 | RAD | $5^7/_8$–$5^{15}/_{16}$ | 46,300 × 2,100 |

A One-Directional Trade

It is important to note that the reason this trade worked out was because it was a completely "one-directional trade." In other words, there was a buying updraft that I rode. This was not a case in which the stock was trading equally back and forth on the bid and the ask. You didn't see prints going $5^7/_8$ . . . $5^{15}/_{16}$ . . . $5^7/_8$ . . . $5^{15}/_{16}$. Instead, it was the exact opposite. The prints went $5^7/_8$ . . . $5^7/_8$ . . . $5^7/_8$ . . . $5^7/_8$ . . . $5^{15}/_{16}$ . . . $5^{15}/_{16}$ . . . $5^{15}/_{16}$ . . . $5^{15}/_{16}$. . . . Once the buyers blew through the $5^7/_8$ stock, there was no turning back. Stock immediately started trading at the next-highest level, $5^{15}/_{16}$.

Please note that I do not advise that you trade 5,000-share lots in the beginning. There is a learning curve involved in these trading strategies, and you will get hurt badly if you try to "size up" before you fully understand how the strategies work and what the risk is. Protect your trading capital during the learning curve. Only trade 100-share lots.

Picking Pennies from in Front of a Freight Train?

One of the main criticisms of this trading strategy is that it is like "picking pennies in front of a freight train." Some will say that you are taking a huge risk to make only pennies on the trade. There is no doubt that this is a big risk to make only a small profit. But guess what? *Day trading is risky!* How are you going to make any money if you don't take risks?

The important thing to remember is that you have to wait until conditions are almost perfect before putting your capital at risk. Anytime you are buying a block of 5,000 shares of stock, this is a very high-risk venture. If the trade goes against you even ¹⁄₁₆th of a point, you will be out $312.50 plus commissions. There is zero margin for error. If you are trying to make ¹⁄₁₆th, you cannot put yourself in a position to lose ¼s and ½s. If you do, you will be out of money fast. So you have to be very careful and watch the stock like a hawk. Always remember that a fool and his money are soon parted. If you are not careful, the market will remind you of that fact very quickly.

In the example I described above, the only thing that shielded me from the risk I was taking was the time frame involved. I bought 5,000 shares of RAD at 2:01, and I sold them at 2:04. Thus I was only "at risk" for three minutes. In addition, you have to ask yourself: How much can the stock really go against me? On a day like this, when Rite Aid is up ¼ point on 7 million shares of volume, the likelihood that the stock would suddenly go from being strong to being weak at the exact moment that I own 5,000 shares is highly unlikely. But there are no certainties in trading. This is a numbers game and you have to go with the best odds. In this case, I was well aware of the level of risk I was taking, and I felt comfortable with that.

Grabbing Dollars from in Front of a Tornado?

In judging the risk/reward of this day trading strategy versus the others mentioned in this book, you have to ask yourself the following question: If trading a stock like Rite Aid is like "picking pennies from in front of a freight train," what is the analogy for trading a momentum stock like Vertical Net or Rambus? *Wouldn't that be like grabbing dollars from in front of a tornado?* Is that a more prudent way to risk your money? If you are putting $30,000 of trading capital at risk, what is a *safer* play: buying 5,000 shares of a $6 NYSE stock like Rite Aid or buying 100 shares of a $300 NASDAQ stock like Rambus? In both cases, you are risking the same amount of money, but is the risk the same? What gives you the best chance of making a $300 profit? Isn't ¹⁄₁₆th point on 5,000 shares of a lower-priced stock easier to make than 3 full points on 100 shares of a higher-priced stock? Perhaps momentum traders would disagree. I guess it all depends upon your risk profile and the kind of trading that suits your personality.

The thing I like most about this kind of trade is that it lets you know right away if you are on the right side of it or not. There is not much guesswork involved. Either it works or it doesn't. This is not the kind of trade that you hold on to for the entire afternoon, hoping and praying that the market will go your way. If it starts to go against you, do not hang around! Get out, take your lumps, and move on to a better opportunity. In fact, the rule of thumb that I use for myself is, the longer the sell order sits unexecuted, *the less likely the trade will go my way.* If, after several minutes, the buying momentum subsides and the stock looks like it is headed lower, I have absolutely no qualms about taking a $\frac{1}{16}$th-point loss. I hate to lose $312.50 (before commissions), but that is far better than losing several thousand in a worst-case scenario if the stock really begins to reverse course.

Sit on Your Hands and Endure "Mind-Numbing" Boredom

The other important aspect of the "lift and place" is being very selective about which opportunities you risk your hard-earned trading capital on. The market does not give money away. The only way you will be able to end up with more money at the end of the day than you started with at the beginning of the day in this trading strategy is to "sit on your hands" and wait until the odds are overwhelmingly in your favor. This could mean literally having to endure the "mind-numbing" activity of watching for hours every single trade in a stock like Rite Aid before getting involved. That is the level of discipline it will take for this trade to work successfully.

If the Stock Is Dead, You Are Dead

Another piece of advice that applies well to the "lift and place" is the selection of the stock. The stock must be in a temporary uptrend. *If the stock is dead, you are dead.* You need buying pressure to create a short-term updraft, and if that buying pressure subsides before you sell your stock, you will be in trouble. For instance, if Rite Aid was down ⅛th of a point on the day, and was trading low volume, I wouldn't touch it. There are too many other places to employ my trading capital.

Are You Paying the Spread on This Trade?

You may be raising the following question: Aren't you breaking one of the cardinal rules of day trading because, in the lift and place, you are actually paying the spread? To initiate this trade, don't you have to lift an offer? The answer is that, yes, you are paying the spread on the way in. However, as much as you are paying the spread on the way in, you are using that same spread to your advantage on the way out (provided, of course, that the trade goes your way).

Why Not Hold Out for an Eighth- or a Quarter- Instead of Just a Measly Sixteenth-Point Profit?

If you happen to catch one of these stocks on a day when it is really moving, you may want to "hold out" for an ⅛th or ¼th point before selling. Be forewarned, however, that anytime you try to make more than a ¹⁄₁₆th in one of these stocks, it is *a bet outside the parameters of supply and demand.* You will get burned if you try to do this too many times, because you will end up taking a loss or breaking even on a trade when you could very easily have made a ¹⁄₁₆th instead. Think about it. How does anyone know that a stock trading at 6 right now will be at 6½ by the end of the day? It could trade to 6½, but couldn't it also go down to 5½? Do you want to risk that when you are sitting on 5,000 shares? Remember, it is not the scalp trader's job to try to outsmart the market and predict what a stock will do four hours from now. Instead, it is about exploiting temporary supply and demand imbalances in the market right now.

In addition, if the stock continues to go higher after you have locked in a ¹⁄₁₆th-point profit, there is no harm in buying it back and repeating the trade at a higher price. For instance, imagine that, after I sold Rite Aid at 5¹⁵⁄₁₆, it went straight to 6¼. Think of how great it would be to make a ¹⁄₁₆th two or three separate times in that updraft! That would be the best of both worlds: making a nice chunk of change, but doing it in such a way that your risk is limited. Think of it this way: Trying to hold out for more than a ¹⁄₁₆th or an ⅛th on one of these "lift and place" trades is the equivalent of trying to hold a NASDAQ stock like Ariba for 10 points. It is a bet outside the parameters of supply and demand. You may get lucky, but you do not want to rely upon luck to make a living.

You must remember that this is not the NASDAQ. You are not going to get a 1- or 2-point move in these kinds of stocks in a matter of minutes or seconds. In fact, you are not even going to get a ½-point move. If you did, there would be no need to trade 2,000- or 5,000-share lots. In fact, if there was that kind of volatility, I would avoid using this strategy at all cost. I would never want to expose myself to that level of risk with a large block of stock.

What Is the Real Risk Involved in the "Lift and Place"?

You may get the impression from the above examples that the "lift and place" is very easy to do. I don't want you to have that in your head. This is a difficult trading strategy that works very well when all of the right conditions are in place. But what happens when the right conditions are not in place? Is it still as easy to make a ¹⁄₁₆th? The answer is no.

There is one fundamental risk factor that you will encounter during the "lift and place" that we have not talked about yet. And this is a risk factor that can make the situation perilous for you if you are not careful.

The risk is that you do not know how much stock the specialist has for sale at the next-highest price level. Let me explain. Remember when we said that only the specialist knows the depth of the market? This means that, when we see a stock trading 6 to $6\frac{1}{16}$, we have no idea how many sell orders are sitting on the books up at $6\frac{1}{8}$. Why does that matter? Because, if we buy stock at $6\frac{1}{16}$, we will need to sell it up at $6\frac{1}{8}$. What is a better situation for us if we have 5,000 shares to sell at $6\frac{1}{8}$: that there are 100,000 shares already on the books for sale at $6\frac{1}{8}$, or that there are only 1,000? Would you rather get behind a 100,000-share sell order, or behind a 1,000-share sell order? In which instance is our sell order most likely to trade? Obviously, you do not want to see a massive amount of stock for sale at $6\frac{1}{8}$ because the more stock on the books for sale, the longer the line we have to get behind.

FLYING BLIND

The risk of the "lift and place" is not knowing how much stock is for sale at the next-higher price level. Only the specialist has access to this privileged information.

RAD $\qquad$ $5\frac{13}{16}$–$5\frac{7}{8}$ $\qquad$ 100,000 × 5,000

When the scalp trader lifts the remaining 5,000 shares at $5\frac{7}{8}$, in a sense he is flying blind. He has absolutely no idea what is in store for him at $5\frac{15}{16}$. Are there 100,000 shares for sale at $5\frac{15}{16}$? Are there 1,000?

Scenario A:

RAD $\qquad$ $5\frac{13}{16}$–$5\frac{15}{16}$ $\qquad$ 100,000 × 100,000

Scenario B:

RAD $\qquad$ $5\frac{13}{16}$–$5\frac{15}{16}$ $\qquad$ 100,000 × 1,000

These two scenarios in Rite Aid paint two entirely different supply and demand pictures. The scalp trader who is long 5,000 shares at $5\frac{7}{8}$ would much prefer situation B to situation A. Look at the ask size at $5\frac{15}{16}$. The scalp trader would be in a much better situation if he only had to get in line behind 1,000 shares at $5\frac{15}{16}$ than if he had to get in line behind 100,000.

As you can see, that is the main risk of the "lift and place." You will never know what the supply and demand situation is like at the next-highest price level. This is exactly why you need heavy institutional buying and large 10,000- and 20,000-share prints to move the market for you. As we have said, the stocks suitable for the "lift and place" trade are extremely liquid, so 100,000 shares can very easily trade, provided of course that the institutions are there greedily buying up the stock.

Adjust This Strategy to the Hot Stock of the Day

This trading strategy can be tailored to any stock on the New York Stock Exchange that is low priced, and trades decent volume, on a day when it is strong. As an offshoot of this, you may want to try this strategy with slightly less active stocks like Raytheon (RTN.B), Kroger (KR), or Philip Morris (MO) on a day when they are in an uptrend. Just like the examples cited earlier, keep in mind that you need institutional buying to make this trade work. If the institutional buyers aren't there, the stock will go nowhere.

Other Areas of the Scalp Trader's Universe

It is important to keep in mind that scalp trading encompasses a wide variety of trading strategies on the New York Stock Exchange, and what we have mentioned here are only two of the many approaches to the game of making razor-thin profits. In the next chapter we will look at an entirely different area of the scalp trader's universe: the world of trading illiquid stocks.

For more information on the lift and place and other cutting-edge strategies for trading NYSE Stocks, including how the specialist manipulates stock prices, consult *The Day Trader's Survival Guide Video Companion.*

8

Moving the Market: The Scalp Trader and the Art of Trading Illiquid Stocks

There is a rare breed of scalp trader (myself included) who tends to gravitate toward the least volatile segments on the New York Stock Exchange. Some of the stocks in these quiet and overlooked market segments may trade only 20,000 shares or less in a single day, and are so "thin" that even a single 3,000-share buy or sell order can literally "move the market." Why do some scalp traders bother trading these illiquid stocks? Because there is money to be made in these issues! In fact, one of the best-kept secrets on Wall Street is that the odds of a profitable trade are higher in these illiquid stocks than in any other segment of the marketplace.

In the last chapter we touched on the premise that, from the scalp trader's perspective, the less volatile the stock, the greater the chance that the day trader will be profitable. In this chapter we will take that concept to the extreme. We are now going to enter a world where the volatility is so low that, in some stocks, you will be lucky to see an ⅛th-point move *for the entire week*. How is it possible to trade these stocks profitably? How can you possibly make any money in a stock that doesn't move? Why would anyone ever waste their time trying to when there are so many other, better opportunities in other market segments? These are the questions that this chapter will answer.

In the last chapter we introduced you to the concept that you do not need to trade the most volatile NASDAQ stocks to make a living as a day trader. We saw why the New York Stock Exchange offers many lower-risk trading opportunities that NASDAQ does not, and how scalp traders can exploit those situations for profit. You must keep in mind that the New York Stock Exchange is a vast and deep market. There are stocks that trade 20 million shares per day, and then there are stocks that may trade only 20,000. There are some stocks, like Ford, General Electric, and Pepsi, that are household names. And then there are issues like Preferred Income Fund (PFD), and BellSouth Capital Funding (BLB) that very few people outside Wall Street have ever heard of. Why bother with stocks that trade only 20,000 shares in a day? Why trade stocks that so few people are familiar with? *Because there is money to be made in these "overlooked" and illiquid stocks, and that is why we are mentioning them here.*

If there is one general theme that we have emphasized so far, it is that there are many different ways in which the scalp trader can approach the game of making razor-thin profits. Some traders prefer to trade more active issues. However, that doesn't mean that you always need to be where the action is to make money as a scalp trader. Sometimes you can do better by going where the action *isn't*. And this is where the scalp trader who trades illiquid stocks comes in.

The Rules Are Different in the Universe of Illiquid Stocks

The scalp trader who trades these thinly traded stocks has an entirely different mind-set from those who trade the more active issues. This is a universe separate from the stocks we talked about in the last chapter, and there are some fundamental differences in approach. First of all, we must make the distinction between what constitutes an illiquid stock and what doesn't. What are the stocks that are found in this low-volatility universe? These are not the stocks like Rite Aid, Kmart, or Silicon Graphics that we talked about earlier. These are not stocks that trade 4 million shares in a single day. Instead, these are stocks that may trade only 20,000 shares, and some may even trade *less* than that.

ILLIQUID STOCKS ARE VERY DIFFERENT IN STRUCTURE FROM HIGH-VOLUME STOCKS

Below is a comparison of two NYSE stocks on the morning of March 20, 2000. Kmart (KM) is a high-volume stock, and BellSouth Capital Funding (BLB) is a low-volume stock.

| KM | $9\frac{7}{16}$–$9\frac{1}{2}$ | 32,000 × 67,500 | 1,906,200 |
| BLB | $22\frac{11}{16}$–23 | 2,000 × 15,100 | 10,700 |

The difference between how the two stocks trade during the day is like night and day. Notice that, by 11 A.M. Kmart has traded almost 2 million shares. BellSouth, on the other hand, has barely traded 10,000. In addition, notice the bid size and the ask size. KM has 32,000 shares on the bid, and BLB only has 2,000. Also, a liquid stock like Kmart will always trade in narrow, $\frac{1}{16}$th-point spreads between the bid and the ask. An illiquid stock like BLB, on the other hand, will be much "wider," in this case having a bid-ask spread of $22\frac{11}{16}$–23, which is $\frac{5}{16}$ths wide!

Specifically, what stocks constitute the low-volatility universe? Things like debt hybrids, closed-end bond funds, and other "stable" market segments. Keep in mind that these are all New York Stock Exchange stocks. Not one of these issues trades on the NASDAQ. As a general rule of thumb, anything that yields between 5 and 9 percent would be considered to be in this category. These stocks are inherently less volatile because they are long-term "income" plays, and thus are not "growth" plays like those you see on the NASDAQ and the more active areas of the NYSE. In other words, these are the kinds of securities in which conservative investors "park" money for long periods of time because they believe the investment is safe. This area is the polar opposite of the high-flying tech stocks like Vertical-Net and Juniper that we described in the beginning of the book.

Please note that, in this chapter, I tend to use the terms "illiquid," "low volatility," "low volume," and "thinly traded" synonymously. For the purposes of this book, they are the same. As we have said, in market segments like closed-end bond funds and debt hybrids, there are literally hundreds of issues that trade no more than 20,000 shares per day while not having price swings of more than a $\frac{1}{16}$th or an $\frac{1}{8}$th point. Thus any of these adjectives are accurate descriptions of how these stocks trade.

The Purest Form of Betting with the House

The main reason for scalp traders being attracted to this universe of illiquid NYSE stocks is because this is a market segment that is generally ignored by the larger day trading community. In fact, some of these stocks are so slow moving that it actually scares would-be traders away. What these day traders don't understand is that they are ignoring a market segment that is probably easier to trade profitably than any other. *The scalp trader who trades low-volatility NYSE stocks is engaged in the purest form of betting with the house that the marketplace offers.*

One of the great things about trading these thinly traded NYSE stocks is that they are so slow moving that you are at no disadvantage in using a regular online broker to execute your trades. Remember when we said that if you use regular online brokers like Ameritrade, Brown, Suretrade, Datek, or Waterhouse to day trade the most volatile NASDAQ stocks, you are going to have trouble competing against the faster players in the market who are using direct-access systems? That is not true in this area of the NYSE where you are dealing with stocks that don't move more than $\frac{1}{16}$th of a point on some days.

In these trades it is not speed of execution that matters. *Instead, it is the ability to capture the spread.* As we have said before, the online brokers are forced to honor the New York Stock Exchange's fair-order handling rules, and that ensures that your buy and sell orders get properly reflected in the marketplace. In other words, you will get a fair execution, provided of course that you use limit orders. As you know, that is not the case with the more volatile NASDAQ stocks.

Basically, these fair-order handling rules eliminate the low-volatility scalp trader's need to rely on the higher cost of the direct-access trading systems that the faster players use. In this game, by using a Datek, Suretrade, or a Brown, the scalp trader pays around $10 or less for a 5,000-share lot.

This is very powerful because the scalp trader can use the cheap commission to his advantage, provided of course that he uses limit orders and not market orders. Keep in mind that when a trade execution is that cheap, even $\frac{1}{16}$th-point profits become very lucrative.

The Game of Scalp Trading Illiquid Stocks Is a Game of Capturing the Spread

How can you possibly trade a stock profitably if it doesn't ever move? One and only one way: *by capturing the spread.* The scalp trader who trades illiquid stocks is not making a bet on the stock going higher or lower. Instead, he is simply exploiting the difference between the bid price and the ask price.

BLB $22^{11}\!/_{16}$–**23**   **2,000 × 15,100**

In this example, BellSouth Capital Funding, the scalp trader will look to buy 2,000 shares at $22^{11}\!/_{16}$. If he is lucky enough to buy the stock there, he will look to sell it up a $\frac{1}{16}$th or $\frac{1}{8}$th point. If he can buy 2,000 shares at $22^{11}\!/_{16}$, and sell them at $22^{13}\!/_{16}$, he will have made $250 in a stock that didn't move!

As you can see, the only way that profit can be made in one of these low-volatility stocks is by exploiting the difference between the bid and the ask. The irony of this trading strategy is that the profit the scalp trader makes is a profit that is usually reserved for the specialist. The specialist likes to keep the quoted market in these "thinner" stocks as wide as possible because he can have a "field day" at the expense of the investing public. Even if the stock trades only 20,000 shares in a day, if the scalp trader can capture an $\frac{1}{8}$th-point profit on 2,000 shares, he has made himself a nice profit with very little risk. This is exactly what the specialist does all day long.

In the above example in BellSouth, what is the real risk involved in buying the stock at 22¾, as the specialist is doing? It is minimal. The bid–ask spread is an ⅛th point wide, and in a slow-moving stock, that is wide enough to allow the day trader to sell the stock he bought at 22¾ at a higher price. In addition, notice where the other sellers are located. Outside the specialist at 22⅞, there aren't any. (Note: There could be a seller above the market we do not see, but it is inconsequential in this stock because, the chances are, it won't trade higher than 22⅞ anyway.)

You Must Make the Spread in Illiquid Stocks

When we say that this game of scalp trading illiquid stocks is really a game of capturing the spread, we mean it. *If you can't put the spread to your advantage, you will have no way of making money on these kinds of trades!* This should drive home the fact that you must limit orders, and attempt to buy the stock on the bid. Do not ever pay the offer on these trades!

This means that if the stock is bid at 22¾, you enter a buy order for

2,000 shares on a 22¾ limit. In theory, to bid for the stock at 22¾ is a "bet with the house." Why do we consider this betting with the house? *To buy a stock on the bid is to buy it at a slight discount to its market value.* In other words, the odds of turning a profit are with you, not against you. That is why we say that it is actually the purest form of betting with the house that the market will give you. However, this premise only holds true if you refrain from using market orders for these stocks! *If you do use market orders, you will be giving your profit margins away to the specialist!*

THE ADVANTAGE OF CAPTURING THE SPREAD IS AMPLIFIED IN ILLIQUID STOCKS

The difference between making and losing money in the game of scalp trading illiquid stocks rests completely on the ability to capture the spread. If you use market orders, and pay the spread on the way in and on the way out, it will be impossible to turn a profit.

EDL $22\frac{3}{8}$–$22\frac{1}{2}$ $1,000 \times 1,000$

Remember, these low-volatility stocks are not likely to have large price swings. The bid price could very well be the lowest the stock trades all day, and the ask price could be the highest! Thus the only way to buy low and sell high is to buy on the bid and sell on the ask. In our example in ConEdison Quics (EDL), a debt hybrid, it is quite possible that the low of the day will be $22\frac{3}{8}$ (the bid), and the high of day will be $22\frac{1}{2}$ (the ask). The scalp trader who buys at $22\frac{3}{8}$ all day and sells at $22\frac{1}{2}$ makes a very nice profit with very little risk.

Sit in Front of a Computer and Vegetate All Day Long?

One of the main reasons for so many day traders avoiding trading these illiquid stocks is because they don't understand how to make money trading them. But there is also a deeper reason for many traders gravitating away from this area. Some simply think that this market segment is too boring! The reality is that these stocks are so slow moving that you could put a bid in and have it sit there unexecuted for several hours! The only thing I can say about this is that there is no such thing as easy money. I am comfortable putting a bid in and having it sit there all day, unexecuted. Why am I comfortable with that? *Because I know that if I am able to buy it at the price I want, I like my chances of being able to turn a profit.* And if that means having to wait three hours to get a trade executed, so be it! At the end of the day, if I am successful, I will have made a profit by taking about one-tenth the risk that I have to take to make that same profit on the NASDAQ side.

When I say that this is the purest form of betting with the house that the marketplace gives you, I can back it up with my own trading records. There was a six-month span in 1999 in which I made a profit on nearly 87 percent of my trades in illiquid issues. In this market segment I had 1,169 sell transactions, and turned a profit on 1,016 trades, broke even on 112, and lost money on only 41. That translates into 9.5 percent break-even trades, and only 3.5 percent losing trades before commissions. When I have traded more active stocks, like Rite Aid and Kmart, I haven't had anywhere near that high a percentage of winning trades. Remember, as far as the NYSE is concerned, the more volatile and active the stock, the more difficult it is for the scalp trader to trade it.

What was the key to making money on these trades? Two things: *sticking with the right stocks, and using limit orders.* What momentum traders do not understand about this strategy is that my profit margins were razor thin. They were kept to $\frac{1}{16}$ths and $\frac{1}{8}$ths. The same was true on the forty-one trades that went against me. Like my profits, I tried to keep those losses to $\frac{1}{16}$ths and $\frac{1}{8}$ths as well. You cannot make it in $\frac{1}{16}$ths and lose it in $\frac{1}{4}$s and come out ahead. That was the key to my success. It must be said that it takes a certain kind of trader to excel in these illiquid stocks, and it may not be suited to your personality, particularly if you are one of those people who crave more "action." Simply put, it takes a level of patience and discipline that many traders do not have.

You Can Make Money Trading a Stock That Doesn't Move

It is important to note that my profits came not from making market bets that the stock would move higher or lower, but instead from exploiting the difference between the bid price and the ask price. I use this as an example because it is proof that *you can make money trading a stock that doesn't move*. If you can stick with stocks that are stable and slow moving, and avoid ones that aren't, you have the potential to make out nicely by following this game plan.

It is also important to put things in their proper perspective. As we have said before, the scalp trader does not make anywhere near the amount of money that a successful momentum trader can make. You are not going to make $20,000 in a single day following the strategies mentioned here. Although I take great pride in my trading performance for that six-month period, I am also humbled to know that there are successful momentum traders who can literally make more money in a month trading NASDAQ stocks than I could ever hope to make in six months in these illiquid NYSE stocks. However, it is not always about how much money you make. *It is about how much money you make and how much risk you take in the process.* So if I can make $250 on a 1/16th on 4,000 shares of a low-volatility stock like ConEdison Quics (EDL) when I know my downside is limited, that, to me, is a better trade than making $1,000 trading a NASAQ highflier like Rambus, Vert, or Juniper.

The Scalp Trader Cannot Expect to Always Get a Fill in Illiquid Stocks

Again, I don't want to make the mistake of misleading you into thinking that this is "easy money." Like anything else, where there is opportunity, there is also risk. One of the interesting aspects of trading illiquid stocks is that, sometimes, you simply won't buy the stock at the price you want. In other words, if I am trying to buy 2,000 shares of EDL on a 22⅜ limit, it is quite possible that my buy order will sit there all day and not get filled. In fact, I bet that if you reviewed my trading during that six-month period in 1999, of the thousand or so trades that did get executed, there were probably another three hundred buy orders that never traded! This drives home the fact that, in extremely illiquid stocks, the scalp trader cannot expect to always buy the stock at the price he wants. As a rule of thumb, expect that one out of every three limit buy orders you place will never trade.

The skill in this trading strategy is having the insight to know what prices are more likely to get filled and what aren't. In other words, you have to walk a fine line between being aggressive enough to buy the stock at your price, and not being too aggressive to overpay, then be unable to sell for a profit. What good is putting a bid in that is so low no one sells to you? That is why this is as much an art as it is a science.

The Dreaded Partial Fill

In addition, there are some other risks involved in trading illiquid stocks that you don't face anywhere else in the market. Generally speaking, it is not the risk of the stock going against you that is the main issue in this market segment. What is the likelihood of a stock that hasn't moved an ⅛th of a point all week suddenly dropping 1 full point? Slim to none. Thus it is not really the risk of loss that is the primary danger here. Instead, the most troublesome aspect of trading illiquid stocks is something we call "partial fills." Let me explain.

These illiquid stocks are so thinly traded that you may put a bid in for 2,000 shares and end up buying only 400 shares. When you buy 400 shares of a 2,000-share order, that is what is called a "partial fill." In addition, generally speaking, if you do buy all 2,000 shares, it is unlikely that you will buy the whole 2,000-share lot at once. It is quite possible that you could end up buying 2,000 shares in twenty 100-shares pieces! (Keep in mind that, thankfully, even though it took twenty different partial fills to buy 2,000 shares, you only paid one trade commission.)

PARTIAL FILLS ARE A NECESSARY EVIL

Partial fills are a necessary evil in the game of trading illiquid stocks. Basically, these stocks are so "thin" it is unlikely that a 2,000-share lot can be bought all at once.

EDL	$22\frac{3}{8}$–$22\frac{1}{2}$	2,000 × 1,000
EDL	$22\frac{3}{8}$–$22\frac{1}{2}$	1,500 × 1,000
EDL	$22\frac{3}{8}$–$22\frac{1}{2}$	1,000 × 1,000
EDL	$22\frac{3}{8}$–$22\frac{1}{2}$	500 × 1,000
EDL	$22\frac{5}{16}$–$22\frac{1}{2}$	1,000 × 1,000

Instead, as this example in EDL shows, you could end up buying 2,000 shares at $22\frac{3}{8}$ in four 500-share lots. Notice how the bid size changes each time 500 more shares are bought, and then eventually, after all 2,000 shares have been bought, the $22\frac{3}{8}$ bid is gone and a $22\frac{5}{16}$ bid appears.

The risk of partial fills is exactly why you will want to exploit the lower commission cost of a regular online broker instead of a higher-cost, direct-access system. Keep your costs as low as possible. In the unlikely event that you end up buying only 400 shares of a 2,000-share order, if you can sell it for a profit, get rid of it! Clean up your position, and move on to a better opportunity. What is it costing you to get the trade done—$10?

I really don't mind partial fills because, in a sense, they are one of the reasons for scalp traders being able to make a profit in these stocks in the first place. Partial fills are a risk in day trading that you must learn to manage. Think about it for a second. Why was I able to turn a profit on 87 percent of my trades? *Because I was helping to provide liquidity to an illiquid market.* In other words, I was like a "wholesaler." I was buying the stock in small lots, packaging it all together into a nice 2,000-share piece, and then liquidating it in the open market at a higher price. This is exactly what the specialist does all day long in these illiquid issues, and that is how he is able to turn a profit in stocks that may trade only 20,000 shares per day. Remember the golden rule: Be a buyer when the market needs buyers, and a seller when the market needs sellers. This is the name of the game in illiquid stocks.

9

How the Specialist Manipulates Stock Prices to Derail Day Traders

Unfortunately, the NASDAQ is not the only market in which the day trader will encounter price manipulation. Though it is less blatant on the NYSE than it is on the NASDAQ, the specialists also engage in their own forms of "questionable" trading practices. This chapter will examine the ways in which the specialist bends the rules to profit, at the day trader's expense.

When trading any NYSE stock, you must always keep in the back of your mind that the specialist has a trading advantage. As we have said in earlier chapters, this is because he has access to privileged supply and demand information that you and I do not have the luxury of having. What is this privileged information? It is the specialist's order book, which shows buyers below the market and sellers above the market. Only the specialist truly knows if the next move in the stock is going to be higher or lower.

The Specialist Has to Make a Living Too

This is why the specialist has the edge, and this is also why he is sometimes tempted into doing things to a stock that are not in line with the investing public's best interests. Put yourself in his shoes. If you had supply and demand information that no one else had, and you were out there risking millions of dollars of your own trading capital every single day, wouldn't you try to use this information for your own benefit? If you could make an

⅛th or a ¼ point at someone else's expense, probably a day trader's, wouldn't you do it? This is exactly the problem. *The specialist has to make a living, just like you and I do.* He has a mortgage to pay, college tuition, and food that he must put on his family's dinner table. Therefore he will use every possible edge that he can to make a living, even if it means "bending" the rules of fair play in the process. Can you blame him?

The way market manipulation occurs on the NYSE is slightly different from the way it occurs on the NASDAQ. But regardless of that fact, the general theme is exactly the same: *Like the market makers on the NASDAQ, the specialist will make the stock look weak to "shake out" nervous sellers, and he will make the stock look strong to "lure in" greedy buyers.* In a nutshell, he will make a stock look weak when he knows it is strong, and he will make it look strong when he knows it is weak. How does he know that a stock is strong or weak? As we have said, because he sees the order book, and he knows if there is a wall of buyers below the market or a wall of sellers above it.

This is another way of saying that the specialist manipulates the market by appearing as a buyer when he is really a seller, and appearing as a seller when he is really a buyer. Why would he ever go to the trouble of misleading the investing public? For the same reason the market makers on the NASDAQ do: *to trade against the investing public and to make money at their expense.* To understand how this drama plays out in the marketplace, we need to look more closely at the specialist's mind-set.

The Mind-set of the Specialist

In a perfect world, the specialist would fulfill his obligation as a market maker by keeping the market even and orderly. Wall Street, however, does not operate in a perfect world. As we have said before, in the short term the markets are inefficient and can be exploited for profit. The specialist is as much aware of this fact as anyone else. In fact, the only reason the job of the specialist exists in the first place is to smooth out the temporary inefficiencies that inevitably occur in stock trading. When there is a buy imbalance, the specialist is a seller. And when there is a sell imbalance, the specialist must be a buyer.

The problem that the specialist faces is the annoying presence of short-term speculators and day traders "shadowing" his every move. This is very similar to the problem that the large brokerage firms like Goldman Sachs and Morgan Stanley face on the NASDAQ. Successful day traders make money by "trailing" and "mirroring" the smart money. The reality is that the specialist cannot keep the trading even and orderly without becoming his own worst enemy. In this day and age of online trading, a stock that is "even and orderly" would become very easy to predict. And a stock that is very easy to predict quickly becomes inundated with day traders. Too many day traders all doing the same thing make it next to impossible for the specialist to profit in the manner he is accustomed to.

The Specialist Will Create Inefficiencies Instead of Correcting Them

The defense that the specialist has is the ability to manipulate the supply and demand in the stock. *The less predictable he can make the stock, the more the specialist stands to profit, at the expense of both the investing public and the day traders.* It is important to remember that this process is nothing more than "smoke and mirrors," the attempt to make a stock look and act erratic when, in fact, it is not. The goal is to force the day trading public to sell when they should be buying and to buy at the precise time they should instead be selling.

How does the specialist do this? To answer this question, we have to go back to the basics of trading on the New York Stock Exchange. What is the primary measure of supply and demand on the NYSE? What is the primary indicator that short-term speculators react to? *It is changes in the bid size and the ask size.*

If the specialist can show a lopsided market, where more stock is willing to be bought than sold, it will appear to the investing public that the stock is headed higher. And when the investing public reacts to what they see, they flood the stock with buy orders. The specialist uses this process as an opportunity to sell into the very updraft that he has created. He can either (1) liquidate a large or long position, or (2) establish a short position.

The result? The investing public is loading up on the stock at the precise moment that the specialist is dumping it! And as you know, when the specialist is dumping the stock, it is not because he thinks it is headed higher.

Inducing a Liquidity Crunch

One of the main ways the specialist will bend the rules of fair play to achieve this effect is something I call "inducing a liquidity crunch." This kind of scenario plays itself out over and over in the marketplace. Keep in mind that, from the day trader's standpoint, supply and demand move stock prices. What is the easiest way for the specialist to derail day traders? *To alter the perception of supply and demand.* This can have a tremendous impact upon a stock in a very short period of time.

Altering the Perception of Supply and Demand

The specialist's goal in inducing a liquidity crunch is simple: to make it very easy for the day trader to get into the stock, and then to make it impossible for him to get out without taking a loss. This strategy counts on those traders who buy and sell "size"—3,000- , 4,000- , 5,000-share lots. The following is a real-life example of how I lost $2,500 in about three minutes on December 13, 1999.

It is important to note that the kind of stock I am describing in this example trades only about 500,000 shares in a day. Thus it is not the kind of low-volume stock that we described in chapter 8, nor is it the kind of high-volume stock like Kmart that we described in chapter 7. It is fair to say that this is one of those NYSE stocks that falls somewhere in the middle. Please note that, like the earlier chapters on NASDAQ manipulation, it is not my intention to point the finger at any particular specialist. I only write this to alert the day trader to the fact that these antics are practiced frequently on the NYSE. Even though I will use actual price data, I will simply refer to the stock as ZZZ.

A Sign of Strength

I remember being attracted to this particular stock because it looked strong. This was the kind of trade in which I thought I could easily make ¼ point or more. On 5,000 shares, a ¼- point profit is $1,250 before commissions.

Phase 1: The Trap

Here's how the drama played out. The quoted market in ZZZ read as follows:

ZZZ $6^{15}\!/_{16}$–7   10,000 × 5,000

A 10,000-share bid appeared at $6^{15}\!/_{16}$. I was convinced the stock was headed higher, so I made an aggressive move to "lift" the 5,000 shares for sale at 7. The specialist immediately called my bluff, sold me stock at 7, then dropped the market like a rock. The split second that my order was filled at 7, he changed the market to:

ZZZ $6^{3}\!/_{4}$–7   13,600 × 5,000

After I had just bought 5,000 shares at 7, the specialist hammered me over the head with a "double whammy" by: (1) dropping the bid price by $^{3}\!/_{16}$ths, from $6^{15}\!/_{16}$ to $6^{3}\!/_{4}$, and (2) putting another 5,000 shares up for sale at 7. Not even five seconds after I bought my 5,000 shares at 7, the stock went from looking strong to looking incredibly weak. In a flash, I was down ¼ point, or $1,250. This was no accident.

When you are in a tight situation like this, there is absolutely nothing you can do. You are completely at the mercy of the specialist and the market. I was long 5,000 shares, and I was immediately looking at a heavy loss.

Phase 2: The Specialist Made the Floor Fall Out from Underneath the Stock

To my horror, the situation worsened. The specialist added more fuel to the fire by dropping the bid yet again, this time from $6^{3}\!/_{4}$ to $6^{11}\!/_{16}$. Even worse, the 13,600–share bid became 100 shares! In addition, he dropped the ask from 7 to $6^{15}\!/_{16}$.

ZZZ $6^{11}\!/_{16}$–$6^{15}\!/_{16}$ 100 × 1,000

A stock that was very easy to get into now appeared virtually impossible to get out of. Put yourself in my shoes. I had just bought 5,000 shares at 7, and now, if I wanted to, I couldn't even sell more than 100 shares at $6^{11}/_{16}$! On paper, I'm down over $1,500 in the span of only a few seconds.

Damage Control

So what do you do when you are faced with this dilemma? How would you react? Unfortunately, there is really nothing you can do other than try to cut your losses. You do not want the situation to spin completely out of control. Once you know that the stock has gone against you, and that there is absolutely no chance of turning a profit on the trade, you have to get into the mind-set of protecting your trading capital. What if the stock drops to 6? Instead of losing a ¼ or ⅜, how would I feel if I lost $5,000 in a matter of minutes? When do you ever make that much money in that short period of time? Never! That is the point: It never happens that way. As a scalp trader you make a living on $^1/_{16}$ths and ⅛ths, and once in a while you lose it in one large chunk. That is why you must manage the situation, and limit the damage as much as possible. Interpretation: Take your lumps and dump the stock wherever you can find a bid!

Phase 3: The Specialist Delivered the Knockout Punch

The knockout punch was delivered when the specialist dropped the bid even lower, from $6^{11}/_{16}$ to 6½. The specialist had forced my hand, and was finally giving me an exit for my stock.

ZZZ	6½–6¾	5,000 × 2,000

But he certainly wasn't doing me any favors because the exit he provided was ½ point lower than where I'd bought the stock from him seconds earlier! After contemplating my options, and fearing that the stock could go even lower, I reluctantly dumped my shares at 6½.

In hindsight, the toughest question I faced was: Do I sell at 6½, or wait? In the back of my mind, I was fearful that the specialist could drop the stock from 6½ to 6 in a heartbeat if he really wanted to. How can I be certain that the stock is not headed to 6? On paper, I was already down $2,500, and I didn't want to see that snowball into a $5,000 loss. I really had no choice. The specialist forced my hand. So I sold. I hit the 5,000-share bid. It could have been much worse. The 5,000 shares I bought at 7 several minutes earlier were sold at 6½. I lost $2,500 in about 120 seconds.

The Dangers of Being Caught on the Wrong Side of a Liquidity Crunch

This example sheds some light on one of the dangers of trading New York Stock Exchange stocks. No matter how perfect the conditions may be for entering a trade, *if the specialist wants a stock to head lower, he will make it go lower.* The chances are, the specialist probably "shorted" the stock to me at 7. By being short 5,000 shares at 7, the specialist now stood to profit if the stock dropped. In other words, the specialist now had a vested financial interest in guiding the stock lower. And if you are the specialist, the best way to make a stock drop is to cancel your bids and induce a liquidity crunch. As they say, there are two sides to every trade: I bought at 7 and sold at 6½ and lost $2,500. Most likely, the specialist sold short at 7 and "covered" at 6½, and made $2,500 AT MY EXPENSE!

Another frustrating aspect of this trade was that my sell of 5,000 shares at 6½ stood as the "low print" of the entire day. Once the specialist absorbed my 5,000-share sell at 6½, he took the market higher again. I will take comfort in the fact that there was absolutely nothing I would do differently if confronted with this situation again. Just because the stock went higher after I sold doesn't mean that, at that time, and under those market conditions, it was a "bad trade." The stock could very easily have gone down to 6, or even lower. When my hard-earned trading capital is at risk, there is no justification in letting a loss of $2,500 get any larger than that.

Liquidity Crunches Cause Market Collapses

One of the most important conclusions from this is that *it is not always sell-ing pressure that drives a stock lower.* Sometimes it is simply an absence of liq-uidity. When the specialist disappears as a buyer, it only takes one or two small sell orders to drive a stock down ½ point or more. This is what I mean when I say that liquidity crunches can cause market collapses.

If anything, this is an indication of just how important the specialist's role is in keeping the market liquid and orderly. Whether he makes money at the expense of the day trader or not, the specialist has a responsibility to the investing public to keep the volatility down and to keep the trading in the stock "fair." And, as you can see, when he steps away from that respon-sibility, the investing public and the day trader are the ones on the short end of the stick.

It is important to note that there is absolutely nothing *illegal* about what the specialist did to me in this example. I can only speculate that he shorted stock to me at 7 and bought it back from me at 6½. I do not know with 100 percent certainty, and there is no way for me to ever know, simply because the New York Stock Exchange is an anonymous market. Unlike the NASDAQ, you will never know who is taking the other side of your trade.

Why couldn't it have been another day trader who sold me stock at 7, and bought it back from me at 6½? It could have been, but it is highly unlikely. In fact, I would bet the farm on the likelihood that the specialist was the one who took the other side of both of my trades. So why did I lose $2,500 on this trade? In my opinion, I lost money because I was trad-ing off inaccurate supply and demand information. *The specialist did not do his job!* Had the specialist shown what the "real" supply and demand in the stock was, I would never have bought stock at 7. No one in their right mind would ever buy 5,000 shares if they knew the floor on the stock was about to fall out from underneath them!

It is bad enough that the specialist didn't do his job, but there is one aspect of this that is even worse. What is so frustrating about this situation is that the specialist could very well have supported the stock with "legiti-mate" bids at $6^{13}/_{16}$, $6^{3}/_{4}$, $6^{11}/_{16}$, or $6^{5}/_{8}$ if he had wanted to. But he chose not to. Instead, he put in ridiculous 100-share bids on the way down. The specialist wasn't willing to buy any stock on the way down simply because he knew something that no one else knew: *that the stock was headed lower.* Why would he buy stock at 6¾ if he knows he can buy it at 6½? And it was only after the stock had plummeted to 6½ that he was comfortable in stepping up to the plate and showing a 5,000-share bid.

The Sucker

One of the things that I hope this last example shows is that it will not take long to realize that you have been "played" by the specialist. The problem with getting caught in a liquidity crunch is that, by time you realize that you are the "sucker," it is way too late to do anything about it. Your money is already at risk, and you will be stuck watching your losses mount.

Instead of calling it a liquidity crunch, perhaps a more accurate phrase would be "a specialist-induced panic." The day trader will lose money on this trade because of the fear factor. It is very hard to maintain your composure when you have a 5,000-share position that is going against you. When a $1,000 loss becomes a $2,000 loss, the last thing any trader wants is the loss snowballing out of control. So the day trader "takes it right on the chin," as they say. *Hindsight is always twenty-twenty,* and there is always room for second-guessing later. However, when your money is at risk, emotion may cloud your judgment and you may be forced into making a decision that you may later regret. And that is exactly what the specialist is counting on.

10

Arbitrage Trading: Unsustainable Valuations and the Hunt for "Free Money"

Every so often there are opportunities during the trading day when stock prices temporarily get "out of whack." When this happens, there is said to be "free money" in the market, and when there is "free money" to be made, the window of opportunity may only last for several seconds before it is exploited by arbitrageurs and alert day traders. But what makes many of these trades unique is that they are not bets on a particular stock going higher or lower. Instead, they are high-percentage bets that the price difference between two different securities will widen or narrow. Using real-life examples, this chapter will examine the parameters of the "free money" trade, and will provide tips on how the day trader can exploit these inefficiencies for profit.

The Hunt for Free Money

Do you remember back in chapter 8 when we talked about how oftentimes it is not how much money you make on a trade that is important, but instead *how much risk you take in the process?* Keep that theme in the back of your mind, because we are now going to completely switch gears. We are leaving the "boring" domain of conventional trading strategies and entering a place that is so exotic and potentially profitable that it attracts the brightest minds on Wall Street. This is the world of arbitrage trading.

There is no question that, in the short term, the market is inefficient. We have seen, over and over, how the forces of fear and greed can distort stock prices, and how the day trader can exploit this for profit. The arbitrage trader also attempts to exploit market inefficiencies, but he does it in a much different fashion: *Instead of making an outright bet on a stock or the overall market going higher or lower, he will bet that the price difference between two different securities will get larger or smaller.*

Exploiting a Market Inefficiency and Taking Very Little Risk in the Process

In a nutshell, the whole name of the game in arbitrage trading is twofold: to exploit a market inefficiency, and, in the process, to take as little risk as possible. Because of this, arbitrage is probably the "purest" form of trading that exists. If it is done properly, the arbitrageur does not care if the market indexes go higher or lower. The nature of an arbitrage position shields him from any risk associated with that. This is why a true arbitrage trade is considered "free money." You are exploiting a market inefficiency *that is not dependent upon the overall market going higher or lower.* To understand this, we must look at an example.

Raytheon Class A Versus Raytheon Class B

A great example of arbitrage trading on the New York Stock Exchange involves Raytheon, the defense giant. Due to a merger that occurred with Hughes Electronics several years ago, there are two different classes of Raytheon stock that trade: class A and class B. The symbols are RTN.A and RTN.B, both of which trade on the New York Stock Exchange. These two classes of common stock have slightly different characteristics, but for the purposes of arbitrage trading, *they are essentially the same security.* This creates a great opportunity for the day trader to play these two stocks against each other.

Prices Get Temporarily Out of Whack

When you have the same security, there should never be a large gap between how the two stocks trade. This is another way of saying that, when the RTN.As trade higher, the RTN.Bs should also trade higher. And when the RTN.As trade lower, the RTN.Bs should follow suit. In a perfect world, these two Raytheon common stocks would trade in perfect sync. Most of the time they do. *But there are some days when they do not! And that is where the opportunity for "free money" comes in.* If Raytheon A was down ½ point on the day, common sense would dictate that, if RTN.A and RTN.B are the same stock, Raytheon B would also be down ½ point. They are virtually the same security, so there should never be any discrepancy between the two. Right? Wrong!

Fear and Greed Distort Valuations

The forces of fear and greed sometimes create supply and demand imbalances, and that can distort the price difference between the two. In other words, Raytheon A and Raytheon B sometimes temporarily get "out of whack." And when this happens there is "free money" to be made.

So as a day trader, how do you make money when RTN.A and RTN.B get "out of whack"? As you know, when there is an inefficiency, it is only a matter of time before the market corrects itself. Therefore the only way to profit from this kind of situation is to immediately exploit it when it develops, and then liquidate the position when the market forces finally "right" themselves.

You must keep in mind that RTN.A and RTN.B cannot stay "out of whack" indefinitely. Why not? Because *"free money" does not last forever.* It is unsustainable. Someone will grab it, and then it will disappear. *If you don't grab it, the specialist probably will!* This is what I mean when I refer to the term "unsustainable valuations." The market will always rectify a valuation that is distorted.

A Pocket of Free Money Appeared, and Then Disappeared

On January 24, 2000, a pocket of free money appeared and disappeared in only nine minutes. This was a great opportunity to play the RTN.Bs against the RTN.As. If you had pulled up the quoted market in Raytheon at 3:18, it would have read:

Quote at 3:18 P.M.:

RTN.A $19\frac{1}{4}$–$19\frac{5}{16}$
RTN.B $18\frac{3}{4}$–$18\frac{7}{8}$

Notice that the Bs were down $\frac{7}{8}$ths on the day, but the As were down only $\frac{5}{16}$ths. The prices were temporarily "out of whack" and there was free money to be made.

Quote at 3:27 P.M.:

RTN.A $18\frac{13}{16}$–$18\frac{7}{8}$
RTN.B $18\frac{13}{16}$–$18\frac{7}{8}$

At 3:27, nine minutes later, the RTN.As dropped $\frac{5}{16}$ths to come back into line with the RTN.Bs. The day trader who was quick to react, and place his bet that the price gap between the two would narrow, made at least $\frac{1}{4}$ point of profit in this trade. The opportunity did not last long, however. The free money was created at 3:18 P.M., and captured by 3:27 P.M.

The First Step Is Isolating the Free Money

So how do you profit when the price difference between RTN.A and RTN.B gets out of whack? It is very simple. By going long RTN.A and short RTN.B, or vice versa, going short RTN.A and long RTN.B, depending upon the situation. Let's look at an example. Let's say that you have been watching the two securities all day, and on this particular day, Raytheon As are trading up ¾ of a point at 21, but Raytheon Bs are trading at 20⅜, *and are only up ⅛ point on the day.* First of all, ask yourself if something is "out of whack." How can RTN.A be up ¾ of a point while

RTN.B is only up ⅛ point? Shouldn't RTN.B also be up ¾ point on the day? Yes, it should. I would look at this situation and say: Something has to give! In other words, there is probably "free money" in this trade.

Keep in mind that, when we say there is "free money" in a trade like this, if you are in and out in the same day, you shouldn't be looking to make points on this trade. Remember, don't try to outsmart the market and don't get greedy. In other words, look for ¼s, ⅜ths, and ½s. For the amount of risk you are taking, that is a nice profit.

Think about this situation from a long-term investor's standpoint. If you really like Raytheon, and you know that the Raytheon As and the Raytheon Bs are almost identical securities, which one would you buy? The one that is up ¾ point on the day, or the one that is up only ⅛th on the day? In other words, the cheaper one, or the more expensive one? Obviously, you would be inclined to buy the Bs over the As, until the two valuations came back into line. And so would everyone else. The result? The Bs get bought by the investing public until the price of the Bs comes closer in line with the As. That is why the market always rectifies these kinds of imbalances.

FREE MONEY

Notice the fact that the RTN.As are up ¾ point on the day, but the Bs are up only ⅛th point. These are virtually identical securities. Under normal circumstances, if the As are up ¾ of a point on the day, the Bs should also be up ¾ of a point.

RTN.A	$20^{15}/_{16}$–21	1,000 × 1,000	+ ¾
RTN.B	$20^{9}/_{16}$–20⅝	1,000 × 1,000	+ ⅛

Until the price of the Bs (20⅝) comes back into line with the price of the As (21), it can be said that there is free money in this trade. How do you capture it? By simultaneously buying the Bs at 20⅝, and shorting the As at 21.

Now that we have "isolated" the free money, we have to go out into the marketplace and "capture" it. How do you capture free money? *By simultaneously buying the undervalued security and shorting the one that is overvalued.* In our case, buying the RTN.Bs at 20⅝, and getting short the RTN.As at 21. This is what we mean when we say that this is a "risk-free trade." By establishing a long/short position, basically, you have eliminated your exposure to market risk. Please keep in mind, however, that when we use the term "risk-free," we use it in the sense that it is "market-risk-free." Do not get the impression that there is no way to lose money on one of these arbitrage trades. There is! The trade can go against you if the gap between the two securities widens.

If the Market Crashes, Do We Care?

What if the overall market crashes 400 points today? Or what if good news comes out on Raytheon and both stocks burst higher by 5 points? In either situation, *we don't care!* Remember, we are not betting on Raytheon going higher or lower. Instead, we are betting that the price difference between the As and the Bs will narrow. If the market crashed, it wouldn't affect us at all, because our exposure is perfectly "hedged." In other words, we are both long and short, so a move in either direction doesn't impact our profit or loss at all. Think about it. What if both RTN.A and RTN.B did shoot higher by 5 points? If that happened, we would probably be unharmed. We would probably make a 5-point profit on the RTN.Bs while suffering a 5-point loss on the As. Thus it wouldn't matter because the two would offset each other.

Absolute Price Levels Mean Nothing in an Arbitrage Trade

The reason arbitrage trading strategies typically attract the brightest minds on Wall Street is because, if they are done properly, market risk is taken right out of the picture. Many on Wall Street believe that the game of betting on the difference between Raytheon As and Bs getting larger or smaller is a higher percentage play than an outright bet as to whether these stocks will go up or down. In our Raytheon trade, whether both stocks drop 2 points together, or rise 2 points together, it does not matter one bit. What matters is that the price gap between the two narrows. That is the only way we can profit on this trade.

SCENARIO ONE: Both stocks trade higher by 2 points, to 23:
RTN.A Bought 5,000 at 20⅝—sold at 23—profit of $11,875
RTN.A Sold short 5,000 at 21—covered at 23—loss of $10,000
Net profit on arbitrage trade: + $1,875

SCENARIO TWO: Both stocks drop by 2 points to 19:
RTN.B Bought 5,000 at 20⅝—sold at 19—loss of $8,125
RTN.A Sold short 5,000 at 21—covered at 19—profit of $10,000
Net profit on arbitrage trade: + $1,875

As you can see, if both stocks rose 2 full points, to 23, in a market rally, or dropped 2 full points, to 19, in a market sell-off, as long as the price gap between the two narrowed from ⅜th of a point to even, our profit margin would be the same.

It Is Not Finding the "Free Money" But Capturing It That Is So Difficult

Let's say that we were successful in buying 5,000 shares of the Bs at 20⅝, and shorting 5,000 shares of the As at 21. And, for the sake of argument, let's also say that the trade went exactly as planned. By late in the afternoon, the Bs had closed the gap and were trading in line with the As. But our work is not done yet. From the day trader's standpoint, the one thing that makes arbitrage trading so difficult is not the task of finding the "free money" (there are numerous times throughout the trading day when arbitrage trades are possible), but, instead, attempting to *successfully unwind the position*. This is the biggest challenge, at the end of the trade.

Thus it can be said that, if finding the free money is not the difficult part, actually "capturing" it is. Even if the trade goes 100 percent according to plan, things can still go drastically wrong if you are unable to get out of the long and the short positions successfully. If you are long 5,000 shares of one stock, and short 5,000 shares of the other, if you don't have the skill and the precision to know how to exit the trade, you could end up completely blowing all of the profit that this trade gave you simply because you had bad executions on the way out.

As it stands, we are long 5,000 shares of RTN.B at 20⅝, and we are short 5,000 shares of RTN.A at 21. Assume that, at this point in the day, both the As and the Bs are finally trading in sync. We face a dilemma: Even though the trade is "in the money," we haven't made a dime until we can unwind both sides of the trade to "lock in" the profit.

It is important to note that in the beginning I do not suggest attempting these arbitrage trades with 5,000 shares. If you get on the wrong side of one of these trades with that kind of size, it could very easily backfire and you could get killed! Respect the learning curve, and "experiment" first with 100-share lots.

The essence of an arbitrage trade is that you unwind both sides of the position simultaneously. In our example, the way to do this would be by (1) selling 5,000 shares of RTN.B to liquidate the long position, and (2) simultaneously buying 5,000 shares of RTN.A to close out the short position. If you are able to successfully liquidate both positions at the same price, you will have locked in a profit of $1,875 (before commissions). Imagining that the market looks as follows, what steps do you take to safely close out this position?

SIMULTANEOUSLY UNWINDING THE TWO-SIDED POSITION

How do you successfully unwind a 5,000-share arbitrage position that is "in the money"?

RTN.B	$21-21\frac{1}{16}$	$5,000 \times 5,000$
RTN.A	$20\frac{15}{16}-21$	$5,000 \times 5,000$

By waiting until the market offers you an exit for both positions. In this case, the quoted market is allowing us to sell the long position and buy back the short position at the same time at the same price. Keep in mind that, in arbitrage trading, paying the spread does not

matter. What matters is getting out of both positions at the same exact time. We can buy 5,000 shares of RTN.A by lifting an offer at 21 while we sell 5,000 shares of RTN.B at 21 by hitting a bid. This is the kind of simultaneous execution that is needed to safely exit this position.

The important thing to remember about arbitrage trading is that when you are betting on a price difference between two securities, you will want to limit your "net" exposure as much as possible. This means that you do not want to run the risk of getting caught in a lopsided position (short more As than long Bs, or vice versa) in the process of trying to unwind both. These two stocks will generally move higher or lower together. If, by mistake, you found yourself being "net long" or "net short," you would be unnecessarily exposed to added risk if the market moved against you.

Any day trader faced with this situation will conclude that arbitrage trading is a very delicate and precise trading strategy. There is simply no room for fear or panic. The notion of isolating and capturing an inefficiency in the market is difficult enough, but it is only one phase of the challenge. As this example shows, unwinding the position can often be the most difficult part.

Please note that between the fall of 1999 and the spring of 2000, I have seen the RTN.As and the RTN.Bs swing from the Bs being $2 more expensive than the As, to the exact opposite, where the As were $2 more expensive than the Bs, and then to both trading back in line. There is the potential that the valuations will stay "out of whack" for extended periods of time before correcting themselves. Keep that in mind when doing these trades.

Sucking Free Money Out of a Stock by "Pinning" the Market

The second exotic arbitrage strategy that I wanted to discuss is called "pinning the market." Unlike the Raytheon trade, when you "pin" the market, you are not betting that the price difference between two similar securities will widen or narrow. Instead, you are concentrating on just one stock, and you attempt to "suck" a $\frac{1}{16}$th point of free money out of it. How do you do this? Basically, by something I call "suffocating" the stock, or *simultaneously buying the stock at one price while you are selling it at another.*

Before we go any farther, I want to warn you that pinning the market is a very dangerous trading strategy. When all goes well, you can make money very quickly and easily this way. It has worked well for me in the past, but this is yet another example of a strategy that can very easily backfire on you if you are not careful. That is why I call it a "suicide trade." It is a high-risk strategy, and it is not suitable for everyone, particularly beginners. To understand the mechanics of this trade, we need to touch upon a few basic principles.

Liquid Stocks Usually Trade in Tight Spreads

An active and liquid stock, like Western Digital (WDC), Kmart (KM), or Rite Aid (RAD), will trade, 95 percent of the time, in tight $\frac{1}{16}$th-point spreads.

| **WDC** | $7-7\frac{1}{16}$ | **100,000 × 100,000** |

The reason for this is that these stocks trade several million shares in a day, so if the spread was wider than a $\frac{1}{16}$th, it would be very easy for short-term speculators to exploit the bid-ask spread for profit. This is another way of saying that there would be "free money" in the stock.

But what happens when a temporary inefficiency arises whereby, for whatever reason, the bid-ask spread becomes $\frac{3}{16}$th wide? Remember, markets are inefficient and valuations do get "out of whack."

The Two-Sided Market Becomes Ours

The reason this trade is so successful is because we are beating the specialist at his own game. In a sense, by pinning the market, we are "strong-arming" the specialist and taking him right out of the stock. This is how we suffocate the stock, by preventing the specialist from buying stock at 7 or selling stock at $7^{1}/_{16}$ until we are completely out of the picture. Think about it. The specialist is required to let customer orders go in front of his own. We are completely exploiting that rule by putting a buy order at one price and a sell order (short) at another. The result? *The two-sided market becomes ours, not the specialist's!* We are the buyer at 7 at the same time that we are the seller at $7^{1}/_{16}$. This puts us in position to be able to simultaneously buy stock at 7 while we are selling it at $7^{1}/_{16}$.

The Free Money Will Always Disappear

It is important to note that the reward in this arbitrage trade goes to the person with the quickest hands. There may be a window of opportunity of literally two or three seconds to put this trade into place before the stock returns to normal.

WDC	7–7$^1/_{16}$	100,000 × 100,000

When the stock finally does come back into balance, the bid size and the ask size will get large again. Notice that we again have 100,000 shares on the bid and the ask. Thus you may have only several seconds to exploit this inefficiency before the market corrects the imbalance and the free money disappears.

Ex-Dividend Arbitrage

The last exotic trading strategy I will touch upon is called *ex-dividend arbitrage*. This is one of my favorite trading strategies, and what makes it unique is that it is can only be executed at certain times during the year. The essence of this strategy is that you buy a stock on the last day that it trades with its dividend attached, strip the dividend, and sell the stock in the open market the next day without the dividend. This trade can produce a ¼- or ⅜th-point profit with very low risk. You profit by exploiting a valuation inefficiency in a stock's dividend cycle. In other words, you exploit the difference between the stock's price when it trades with the dividend, and its price when it trades without the dividend. To set the background, let's use an analogy.

Imagine that you are in the business of buying and selling leather wallets. The wallets that you "trade" cost you about $49.90 and you typically buy 2,000 wallets at a time and sell them for a small profit up at $50. Also imagine that every wallet you buy comes with a $1 bill inside.

In addition, on the last day of every quarter, assume that the wallets are sold in the marketplace without the $1 bill inside. You buy the wallets at $49.90, pocket the $1 bill inside, then sell the wallets in the open market.

Because you "trade" these wallets every single day, you are one of only a handful of people who know that the $1 bill is no longer in the wallet. Your customers are accustomed to seeing a $50 price tag on this wallet, but on this day, because the $1 bill is not inside, you mark the wallet down. But there is a secret here. You do not lower your price by $1. *Instead, you lower it by only 50 cents!* The result? The public thinks the wallets are on sale because you are selling them today at $49.50 and you sold them yesterday at $50, and thus they snap them up. *What they don't know is that your profit margin is actually 50 cents higher today than it was yesterday, even though you are selling the wallets at a slightly lower price!* This is exactly how I profit when I do an ex-dividend trade.

If you take a stock like ConEdison Quics (EDL), this high-yielding debt hybrid pays roughly a 50-cent dividend four times per year. The day the stock trades without the dividend (ex-dividend) is the thirteenth of every third month, in other words, March 13, June 13, September 13, and December 13. If the stock is trading around $25, this means that if you buy the stock on March 12 at $25, you will get roughly a 50-cent dividend deposited into your brokerage account for every share you buy. Thus if you buy 2,000 shares, you can expect almost $1,000 in dividends ($970, to be exact). The brokerage firm will deposit the dividend in your account on the dividend pay date, which is usually the thirty-first of the month following the ex-dividend date.

The reason this trade works is because, when the stock trades for the first day without the dividend, *the specialist reduces the price accordingly*. For instance, if the stock closes on March 12 at 25, he will open the next day at 24½ because it is no longer trading with the dividend. What I do is buy one of these high-yielding stocks like EDL the day before the ex-dividend date, pocket the 50-cent dividend, and then sell it in the open market the next day.

Exploiting the Perception That the Stock Is "Cheap"

The reason this trade works is because the investing public has no idea when the stock is trading with the dividend and when it is not. So when they see EDL trading for weeks around 25, and then they see it suddenly trading at 24½, they think it is cheap! What they don't know is that the value has not changed at all. The only thing that has changed is the fact that it is no longer trading with a dividend. When the investing public sees it at 24½, they start buying what they think is cheap stock. They say to themselves, "The stock was trading at 25 yesterday, so it must be a bargain today at 24½." The result? The public bids the stock up, and you may get a ¼- or a ⅜-point pop.

For instance, assume that I buy 2,000 shares of EDL at 25 on the last day of the dividend cycle. It pays a 48.5-cent dividend per share, so I will get a $970 dividend check deposited in my brokerage account at the end of the month. So my cost for the stock is really only about 24½. To get the dividend, you must hold the stock overnight. When it opens for trading the next day at 24½ (remember, the specialist will reduce the price by the amount of the dividend), if I can sell it at 24¾, I will have made a ¼-point profit on the trade. How did I do that? I lost ¼ on the trade itself (buying at 25 and selling at 24¾), but I made ½ point on the dividend, so I really made a ¼-point profit! This trade works because it exploits a perception that the stock is cheap when it really isn't. I would use this strategy only with things like EDL, BLB, and other debt hybrids.

For more information on ex-dividend, pinning the markets, and other exotic arbitrage strategies, consult *The Day Trader's Survival Guide Video Companion.*

11

Beating the Specialist at His Own Game

If you lose money trading NYSE stocks, the chances are it is not because other day traders are taking your money. The specialist is probably the one beating you. Always be mindful of the fact that, if the specialist is the one taking the other side of your trades, you will probably lose money. As a conclusion to our segment on trading New York Stock Exchange stocks, I thought it would be fitting to put you, the reader, in the specialist's shoes. The first step toward beating your competition is knowing how they think, how they act, and how they trade.

A Perfect World Where Day Traders Don't Exist

Remember, in the chapter on market manipulation, how we criticized the specialist for not doing his job properly? What is a specialist's incentive for bending the rules of fair play and stepping away from his responsibility to the investing public? Obviously, we know that it is to make money. And when the rules are bent, it is unfair to day traders and the investing public and we usually lose money. Obviously, when we lose money it goes out of our pockets and into the specialist's pocket.

How should the specialist do his job if he isn't trying to manipulate the market, and he isn't trying to make money at our expense? What would be a fair market environment, where the individual would have the same opportunity to profit as the specialist? To answer this we have to use another example. This is very important, because before you become "specialist for a day," we have to touch more upon how the specialist "should" maintain the market if we lived in a perfect world. What would be a perfect world? A place where day traders didn't exist, and the specialist was committed to serving the best interests of the investing public at all times. As you know, we don't live in a perfect world.

In a perfect world the specialist system would ensure that the trading in stocks would be even and orderly. In theory, the backbone of an "orderly" market would be twofold: (1) even bid and ask sizes at each price level, and (2) orderly movement in $\frac{1}{16}$th-point increments, regardless of whether the stock trends higher or lower. Let's look at how a liquid stock like Philip Morris "should" move from 22 to $22\frac{3}{16}$:

AN EVEN AND ORDERLY MARKET

In a perfect world the quoted market would always be in balance. For instance, in a liquid stock like Philip Morris (MO), the specialist would slowly accumulate stock at 22, and he would slowly sell shares at $22\frac{1}{16}$.

MO	$22-22\frac{1}{16}$	$50,000 \times 50,000$

Eventually, if the stock was trending higher, the buying public would "clean out," or buy all of, the stock that the specialist had for sale at $22\frac{1}{16}$. The specialist would then adjust the market $\frac{1}{16}$th of a point, to:

MO	$22\frac{1}{16}-22\frac{1}{8}$	$50,000 \times 50,000$

As the stock continued to edge higher, the specialist would now be accumulating stock at $22\frac{1}{16}$ and selling it at $22\frac{1}{8}$. When the public eventually "cleans out" the $22\frac{1}{8}$ stock, the specialist would adjust the market another $\frac{1}{16}$th point higher, to:

MO	$22\frac{1}{8}-22\frac{3}{16}$	$50,000 \times 50,000$

In theory, this kind of quoted market would be very fair to the investing and the day trading public. Notice that the stock moved from 22 to 22³⁄₁₆ in an even and orderly fashion. Each price level had 50,000 shares for sale, giving the investing public ample opportunity to accumulate stock at 22¹⁄₁₆, 22⅛, and then 22³⁄₁₆. The specialist will have done his job by keeping volatility down and supply and demand in check.

The specialist would stand to profit handsomely in the above example because he would be buying and selling "evenly." In other words, he would be consistently buying ¹⁄₁₆th point cheaper than where he was selling *all day long.* In theory, in a stock that traded several million shares, the specialist could make tens of thousands of dollars per day in trading profits.

Getting Boxed Out by the Day Traders

But there is a catch. The specialist would only be able to "print money" this easily if he had no competition, *if and only if day traders didn't exist.* But the specialist does have competition, and unfortunately for him, day traders are everywhere. That prevents the specialist from making the kind of "easy money" that he may have made before the online trading revolution. Keep in mind that, if the trading in the stock was that easy to predict, the specialist would get completely "boxed out" by the day traders. The day traders would be the ones making the ¹⁄₁₆ths on the order flow, not the specialist. Ironically, the day traders would reap the benefits of the orderly market that the specialist provided. Therefore the specialist has to do things a bit differently to keep the day traders "at bay." And as you now know, he keeps them "at bay" through the use of smoke and mirrors.

This is not a perfect world, and therefore liquid stocks, unlike the model above, do not trade in an even and orderly fashion. Instead, the more active stocks move in a choppy fashion, which puts the investing public and the day traders at a severe disadvantage when compared with the specialist. By confusing the trading public, the specialist is able to make money very easily, at the trading public's expense. Let's look at how MO could move from 22 to 22³⁄₁₆ under normal and imperfect trading conditions.

This is very similar to the way in which the market makers manipulate the supply and demand on the NASDAQ. Remember when we said that the easiest way for a market maker to buy stock is to make the stock look weak? The same strategy is true on the New York Stock Exchange. If the specialist knows that the stock is headed higher, he will "bluff" by making the stock look weak to bring out sellers. When the sellers come out, he snaps up all of the cheap stock, and then, when he has bought enough stock, he takes the market higher again.

The specialist now makes three very important, yet subtle, moves. Once he buys enough stock at 22, he moves the market higher by doing three things simultaneously: (1) raising his bid at 22 from 5,000 shares to 50,000 shares, and (2) canceling his sell of 200,000 shares and replacing it with a sell of only 5,000, and (3) raising his sell price from 22$\frac{1}{16}$ to 22$\frac{1}{8}$. Unlike before, there is now more stock that can be bought, and less stock that can be sold. A stock that seconds ago looked like it was headed lower has reversed course and now appears to be heading higher.

Now that the market looks as if it is headed higher, the specialist hopes to "draw" large buyers into the market in the same fashion that he drew sellers into the market seconds earlier. He makes the stock look lopsided. When it does, he will sell 5,000 "measly" shares at 22$\frac{1}{8}$ and then sell as much as he can up to 22$\frac{3}{16}$. Keep in mind that he just bought a ton of stock at 22, so anything that he can unload at 22$\frac{1}{8}$ and 22$\frac{3}{16}$ is pure profit.

THE SPECIALIST BOUGHT STOCK WHEN NO ONE WANTED IT, AND IS NOW SELLING IT WHEN EVERYONE WANTS IT

The investing public reacts to what they see: a stock that seconds ago had 200,000 shares for sale at 22$\frac{1}{16}$ now has only 5,000 shares for sale at 22$\frac{1}{8}$. Less stock for sale, and at a higher price. The buyers rush to get their hands on what they think is cheap stock at 22$\frac{1}{8}$, not knowing that this is yet another illusion created by the specialist.

Third move: MO   22–22$\frac{1}{8}$ 50,000 × 5,000

The specialist bought the stock from the investing public at 22 when everyone thought the stock was headed lower, and is now selling it back to them at 22$\frac{1}{8}$ and 22$\frac{3}{16}$ when they think it is headed higher.

What the investing public doesn't understand is that, as far as the specialist is concerned, the move is over. *The stock will not trade higher than 22³⁄₁₆!* Remember when we said in the first chapter that the investing public's entry into a stock is usually Wall Street's exit? This is a perfect example of that. In the eyes of the specialist, the buyers of stock at 22⅛ and 22³⁄₁₆ are "suckers." In the span of about ten seconds, the specialist was able to buy thousands of shares at 22 and immediately resell them at 22⅛ and 22³⁄₁₆. The ⅛th and ³⁄₁₆th profit he made came directly at the expense of the investing public, who were caught off guard by the "smoke and mirrors" that he created.

Stepping Into the Specialist's Shoes

Now that we have spent enough time examining how the specialist can manipulate the supply and demand in a stock, it is time to put yourself in his shoes. To set the background, we have a strong stock, Cendant (CD), that has a buy imbalance on the open. Our goal, as the specialist, is to use this buy imbalance as a golden opportunity to make money at the expense of the investing public. There are several steps we have to take to accomplish this—and by now you should know what these are.

1. Open the stock at a fair price.
2. Establish a large short position on the open.
3. Manipulate the stock lower and induce panic selling by the investing public.
4. Cover our short position at lower prices for a profit.
5. Buy aggressively at the bottom.
6. Once long, take the market higher and sell into the rally.

It is important to note that this whole drama could play out in a matter of minutes. A specialist who is properly positioned in this situation could make substantial amounts of money within a short period of time.

The stock that you are in charge of trading is Cendant (CD). After the closing bell yesterday, the head of Cendant hinted to analysts that this would be a "blow-out" quarter, that earnings would far exceed expectations. By 9:15 A.M. the next morning, the stock is inundated with buy orders. And by 9:29 your order book looks as follows: (1) 5 million shares to buy "at market," and (2) 3 million shares to sell "at market." If the stock closed at 20, where do you open it?

The Burden of Opening the Stock at a "Fair Price" Rests in Your Hands

You have a big problem on your hands. The stock cannot open until the buy imbalance is rectified. It is your job to "match" all of the buyers with sellers. Both buyers and sellers are entitled to an immediate execution, provided of course that the orders were entered at "market." In fact, it would be illegal for you to open the stock without giving each "market" order the opening "print," regardless of whether there is a buy or a sell imbalance. So if you open the stock at 25, all buyers and sellers must receive that price.

This is where you earn your paycheck. The burden of opening the stock rests firmly on your shoulders. The specialist has a responsibility to the investing public to give them a fair price. But at the same time, if his own trading capital is at risk, the specialist also has to be mindful of his best interests. This will exert a strong influence on where the stock opens, and how it trades in the minutes that follow.

The problem is that there are 2 million more shares that can be bought than sold. To further add to the dilemma, your position in Cendant is "flat." In a perfect world, if you were carrying a few million shares "long" from yesterday's trading, opening the stock would be very easy. You would sell your 2 million shares to the excess of buyers on the opening "print," and that would rectify the buy imbalance. But you do not have that luxury. So the only way you can open the stock for trading is to become the seller of last resort. Because you don't own any stock, you will have to "short" 2 million shares to the public.

So where do you open the stock? And how do you determine, as the specialist, what is a fair price? You are mindful of the substantial risk involved in taking a 2 million share short position. From your standpoint, this huge risk will undoubtedly be a factor in determining where you open the stock. The problem you face is cut and dried: Until you can cover your short, *you must make sure the stock doesn't trade any higher than the opening price.* If it does, you could lose millions of dollars today.

Let's examine this in more detail. This is a very perilous situation for you, the specialist, to be in. It is 100 percent in your best interests to do two things: (1) to open the stock abnormally high, and then (2) to try to guide it lower after the opening print. Imagine if you open the stock at 23, and then it immediately runs to 24. Because you would be short 2 million shares at 23, on paper you will have lost $2 million! Therefore, to protect yourself, it is imperative that you open the stock so high that it "over-shoots" the market.

This shows us that, from the standpoint of the specialist, the most important factor in this trade is not where the stock opens, but *what the stock does in the seconds and minutes after it opens.* As the specialist it doesn't really matter to you if you open the stock at 24, 25, or 26. What does matter to you is that, regardless of where it opens, it must start to head south immediately so that you can cover your short at a profit.

Manipulating the Supply and Demand to Make a Strong Stock Look Weak

Based upon your knowledge, instinct, and years of trading experience, you decide to open the stock at 26. Thus you are short 2 million shares at 26. What do you do next? The stock absolutely, positively cannot trade higher than 26. If it does, you will be buried alive. So you have to do everything in you power to make the stock look weak. Your livelihood and the preservation of your trading capital depend upon it.

So how do you make the stock look weak? The answer is very simple. You manipulate the supply and demand to give off the illusion of selling pressure. By doing this, you hope that the investing public reacts by dumping the stock. This way, if the selling pressure accelerates, it will give you the opportunity to cover your short position at lower prices. Instead of losing several million dollars, if the stock trends lower you could very easily make several million. Remember, you are short 2 million shares at 26. If you could cover that short position at an average price of 25½, that is a cool $1 million in trading profits for a few minutes of work!

As we have learned, making the stock look weak is a three-step process: (1) making the opening print the offering side of the market, (2) showing large amounts of stock for sale on the offer, and (3) showing very little buying support with a small bid.

A Lopsided Market

Mere seconds after the stock opens at 26, the specialist (you) shows a lopsided market. There are 10,000 shares on the offer, but only 500 on the bid. You hope that the investing public reacts by selling.

| CD | $25^{13}/_{16}$–26 | 500 × 10,000 |

It is important to note that the 10,000 shares you have for sale at 26 are actually a "short" offer as well. Remember, you are short the stock already. Under no circumstances do you want that stock to trade at 26. If it does, you will have added to your short position, which is the last thing you want to do after being short 2 million shares. This is one of the perils of trying to manipulate the market lower. There is always the risk that the attempt to manipulate the market lower could backfire.

In addition to making the market lopsided, there is another subtle move that was made. You opened the stock on the offering side of the market. In other words, you made the opening print occur on the offer, not the bid. This is a very subtle, but influential, move. Think about it: If a 5 million–share buy order can't make the stock trade higher than 26, what can? This stock is headed lower.

The goal of all of the smoke and mirrors is to get the investing public to start dumping the stock. That will be your only opportunity to cover your short position. Remember, covering your short means that you have to buy back 2 million shares. The only realistic chance for you to accumulate that much stock is to buy on weakness. If the stock gets strong again, you are dead! So the last thing you want is for the day traders to start buying the stock before it comes in. To protect yourself, you guide the stock lower by keeping the market lopsided and making it look as though it is weighed down. Here is how it appears:

Phase 1:	$25^{13}\!/_{16}$–26	500 × 10,000
Phase 2:	$25^{11}\!/_{16}$–$25^{7}\!/_{8}$	500 × 10,000
Phase 3:	$25^{5}\!/_{8}$–$25^{13}\!/_{16}$	500 × 10,000
Phase 4:	$25^{1}\!/_{2}$–$25^{11}\!/_{16}$	500 × 10,000

If you can keep displaying these lopsided markets, it will inevitably bring out sellers. But you have to use the opportunity to be an aggressive buyer, buying heavily on the way down at $25^{13}\!/_{16}$ . . . $25^{3}\!/_{4}$ . . . $25^{11}\!/_{16}$ . . . $25^{5}\!/_{8}$ . . . $25^{1}\!/_{2}$ . . . $25^{3}\!/_{8}$. Buying on the way down, however, is not as easy as it looks. Remember, you have day traders actively watching your every move. *You cannot show large bids!* If you do, the day traders will start bombarding the stock with buy orders. Thus the only way you are going to be able to fool the market is to show very small bids even though you are an aggressive buyer. If the investing public knew you were buying all the stock in sight, the panic selling would dry up and other buyers would come into the market. Therefore, the strategy must be kept "under wraps."

One of the advantages of being the specialist is having the ability to buy more stock than your bid shows. For instance, if you show only a 100-share bid, but a 10,000-share sell order comes in, as the specialist you are at liberty to buy all 10,000 shares if you want. In a sense this is similar to the way the market makers on the NASDAQ manipulate the market by showing only a 100-share bid and buying tons of stock at that price. However, keep in mind that, unlike the NASDAQ, it is rare when the specialist actually uses this rule to his advantage.

Please note that if you are willing or I am willing to buy stock at 25½, and a seller comes in, it is perfectly legal for the specialist to jump ahead of us and buy the stock for himself provided that he pays the seller a higher price. I could bid 25½ and the specialist could actually snap up all of the stock himself by paying 25⁹⁄₁₆. How is that fair? Because the seller is actually getting a price improvement, receiving 25⁹⁄₁₆ on the sale of his stock instead of 25½, which is what he would get if it was sold to a day trader instead.

The day trader does not have the luxury of being able to exploit this rule. The only way you or I could buy 10,000 shares is by showing a 10,000-share bid. This is clearly one of the advantages that the specialist has over the investing public. This edge is the "trump card" that will allow the specialist to show a weak market while at the same time being an aggressive buyer.

THE TRUMP CARD

How is the specialist able to conceal the fact that he is an aggressive buyer? As this example shows, by showing a small bid while simultaneously buying all of the stock in sight.

CD   25⅝–25¹³⁄₁₆ 100 × 10,000

It is not illegal for the specialist to do this. If a 10,000- or 20,000-share sell order comes in "at market," he is at liberty to buy the whole piece at 25⅝, even though he is only showing a bid for 100 shares.

The Specialist's Worst Nightmare: A Hedge Fund Enters the Market

To add more fuel to the fire, let's say that a large hedge fund is watching your actions very closely. This hedge fund is interested in buying 50,000 to 100,000 shares this morning. Hedge fund managers are the brightest minds on Wall Street, and they are not easily fooled. In this case this fund is on to your game, and is fully aware that you are trying to manipulate the market lower simply because you need to cover a large short position. Like the specialist, large hedge funds will typically accumulate stock on weakness, not strength. This is because they have huge pockets and virtually unlimited buying power. In this case the lower the stock goes, the more interested in it this hedge fund becomes. When it gets to a 25⅝ bid, the fund enters a 20,000-share buy order.

This could create a major problem for you. What is the one thing that can stand in the way and prevent the specialist from covering his stock? An influx of customer buy orders. This would be your worst nightmare because it would interfere with your ability to cover your 2-million-share short position. The rules of the exchange state that the minute buyers show up, the specialist is forced to give them priority. No matter how much you want or need to buy stock, the customer orders always go first.

A Problem for the Specialist

When a large buyer or group of buyers comes into the market, the specialist will not be able to cover his stock until they are out of the way. In this example, a hedge fund wants 20,000 at 25⅝.

CD $25\frac{5}{8}-\frac{13}{16}$ **20,000 × 10,000**

The specialist cannot do anything but give the order priority, no matter how badly he needs to buy stock. This is a double whammy. In addition to interfering with the specialist's ability to buy stock, this large buy order will also screw up the specialist's attempts to make the stock look weak.

Front-Running the Hedge Fund Buy Order Under the Guise of "Price Improvement"

In the event that this kind of scenario does present itself, the specialist has a few "tricks" up his sleeve that will allow him to buy stock ahead of the hedge fund. As we have said, if a customer buy order shows up as the highest bid, it would be illegal for the specialist to "front-run" the order and buy stock at the same price. It doesn't matter if it is an individual investor or the largest hedge fund in the world. In our example, under no circumstances is the specialist allowed to buy stock at $25\frac{5}{8}$ until the hedge fund order is canceled, or filled.

CD	$25\frac{5}{8}$–$25\frac{13}{16}$	$20{,}000 \times 10{,}000$

If the specialist is aggressive and smart, he will get around this front-running rule by utilizing an age-old Wall Street trick. He will "front-run" the hedge fund by "paying up" for the stock, as we explained earlier. For instance, in the above example, if a 10,000-share sell order came in "at market," it would be perfectly legal for the specialist to grab the stock ahead of the hedge fund by paying up a $\frac{1}{16}$th. How is this done legally? By paying $25\frac{11}{16}$! In other words, the specialist does this by outbidding his own customers.

In a sense, the specialist is "front-running" the hedge fund. However, in the eyes of the exchange and the regulatory agencies, it is perfectly okay because the specialist gave the seller a better price by $\frac{1}{16}$th of a point. In other words, the specialist provided "price improvement." The fact that the hedge fund wasn't able to buy any stock at $25\frac{5}{8}$ is inconsequential. The specialist will use this strategy anytime he finds himself in a "short squeeze."

The Closest Thing on the NYSE to a "Hidden Order"

Earlier in the book we talked briefly about the use of "hidden orders" on the NASDAQ market. These are buy and sell orders day traders use that are hidden from view but actually do exist in the marketplace. These orders are not allowed on the NYSE. However, it is ironic that what is occurring here is essentially a variation of this. By reflecting the hedge fund's bid at 25⅝ in the quoted market, the specialist fools the hedge fund. He gives the hedge fund the false impression that it is the highest bid in the market. Obviously, it is not. *The specialist will not let the hedge fund buy stock, because he will snap it up for himself by paying a higher price!* Remember the old rule: When the true supply and demand in the stock is hidden from view, the investing public is at a severe disadvantage. At this point in the day, the quoted market is somewhat misleading. *This only happens when the specialist has an ax to grind.* Just think of the disadvantage that this places the hedge fund under. They have absolutely no chance of buying stock at 25⅝, simply because the specialist will not let them. Worst of all, they don't even know it.

If the hedge fund knew that the specialist was secretly bidding $25^{11}/_{16}$, they wouldn't sit back at 25⅝. They would probably raise their bid to 25¾, $1/_{16}$th point higher than the specialist's bid. Keep in mind that the specialist, being short 2 million shares, does not want the market to "creep" higher. This is exactly what would happen if the specialist got in a "bidding war" with the hedge fund.

There is another irony in this situation. The specialist will not let stock trade at 25⅝ as long as a customer order is there. However, if the hedge fund wasn't there, I guarantee that the specialist would not be paying $25^{11}/_{16}$ to accumulate stock. Instead, he would be buying it at lower prices—25⅝, $25^9/_{16}$, or even lower. The specialist is obviously not stupid, and is not in the business of leaving money on the table. He only "pays up" when he is forced to. The conclusion is that it is perfectly okay for the specialist to buy stock at 25⅝ or cheaper, but it is not okay for the investing public to do the same. It only drives home the fact that, when all is said and done, the specialist is in the business of trading against his customers.

To take this example to the extreme, let's say that you were able to buy back all 2 million shares at prices lower than 26. In fact, in addition to covering your short, you added to the position and are now "net long" 200,000 shares of the stock. What is the next move? In the same way that you took the stock lower, you will now take it higher. Before, because you were short, you had a vested interest in guiding the stock lower. But now, because you are long, the tables have turned. You have a vested interest in manipulating the stock higher.

The Stock Will Trend Higher or Lower Depending Upon Whether the Specialist Is "Net Long" or "Net Short"

That is the wisdom of this example. As we have said over and over, the day trader must trade with the ebbs and flows of the specialist. These ebbs and flows are determined not by market fundamentals, but by the nature of the specialist's trading account. The specialist will sell strength and will buy weakness. As we have also said over and over, if you can overcome his smoke and mirrors and sell when he is selling and buy when he is buying, over time you will be a winner.

This example also drives home the fact that, in the more active stocks, the day trader must be looking to buy a strong stock on the pullback. You now know that the "hand" you are playing in a strong stock is the fact that the specialist is short. So you wait for the stock to pull in and you jump aboard. At that precise moment, when the stock stops falling, that is a clear indication that the specialist is having difficulty "covering."

If you can buy then, the stock has nowhere to go but up. And if your prediction comes true and the stock begins to rally, this will put the specialist in a tight spot. He needs stock to cover his short, and if he can't get it he will be looking at a large loss. This can very quickly turn the specialist into a "panic buyer." To add fuel to the fire, the day traders, the hedge funds, and the investing public will join the feeding frenzy, tripping over each other to chase the stock. The result? The stock will surge higher. The day trader who was buying stock on the pullback is now looking at a nice profit. Case closed.

12

A Utopian Vision for a Fair Marketplace: The Twenty-Four-Hour Unified Exchange, the Virtual Specialist, and the Extinction of Traditional Wall Street

"The ability of all investors to see the depth of the supply and demand in any stock would be a giant step towards a true national market system."

—ARTHUR LEVITT, CHAIRMAN
Securities and Exchange Commission, The New York Times, March 17, 2000.

If the present-day NASDAQ and NYSE were truly fair to the investing public, would seven out of ten day traders still be losing money? Why is it that both the NYSE and the NASDAQ claim to be serving the best interests of the general public, yet neither has made any serious effort to make the kind of changes that truly would level the playing field for the individual? The answer is that, if the NYSE and the NASDAQ did make those changes, they would be hastening their own extinction. I can envision a world in the near future in which day traders would truly be on a level playing field with Wall Street. For this to happen, the NASDAQ system as we know it has got to go.

I want to conclude this book by addressing a very relevant and controversial topic in today's marketplace. There is no doubt that the future of the NASDAQ, the NYSE, and electronic trading in general will be some sort of a twenty-four-hour unified exchange. We are already seeing a glimpse of this with the growth in after-hours trading. With the inevitable changes that lie ahead, what would be the fairest market mechanism from the standpoint of the individual investor and the day trader? What would ensure that we get the best possible execution? This chapter will answer these questions.

Wall Street Knows the Present System Is Not Fair to The Investing Public

I'm sure you have seen over and over in the media how both the NYSE and the NASDAQ claim to have the best interests of the investing public in mind. How can the NYSE and the NASDAQ claim to have the best interests of the investing public in mind while allowing an uneven playing field for everyone other than the market makers and the specialists, particularly day traders? Isn't this a contradiction?

So the million-dollar question is: *How do you level this playing field?* The answer is that you get rid of the "old guard" rules that have allowed Wall Street to make so much money for decades at the expense of the investing public. By scrapping the old system, you create a new, fair system in which the general public has the same access to the "true" supply and demand information in a stock that the major financial institutions do. This would effectively eliminate the inherent disadvantage that the day trader faces when competing with the Wall Street pros.

The Virtual Specialist

How could this be done? I argue that the mechanism would be a kind of "virtual specialist system," a combination of the best aspects of both markets: the transparency and depth of the NASDAQ Level II and the "fairness" of the specialist system on the NYSE. The irony is that if the

NASDAQ and the NYSE truly have the individual investors', and not Wall Street's, best interests in mind, putting these innovations in place would ultimately lead to their own extinction. Think about it. Why would you need NASDAQ anymore? And, if everything was done electronically, why would you even need a "floor" like the NYSE? You wouldn't need either. These people would all be out of jobs. That is why the establishment has been so reluctant to embrace any changes.

The first step in this process of change would be to entirely scrap the NASDAQ market-maker system as we know it. It is not a fair system. The only redeeming quality of the NASDAQ system is being able to see the depth of the market. Who are the buyers below the market, and who are the sellers above the market? Other than that, as we have seen in this book, it is an extremely fragmented and unfair market that favors the member firms at the expense of the investing public.

Imagine, for a second, the prospect of taking all of those NASDAQ stocks and listing them on some sort of centralized, electronic "specialist's book." In the process you would put all of the market makers out of work. The burden to provide liquidity in these stocks would no longer rest in the market makers' hands. It would become the specialist's job. If a Wall Street brokerage firm like Goldman Sachs or Merrill Lynch wanted to buy or sell the stock, they would have to do so the same way that you and I do: They would have to get in line at a particular price on the specialist's order book. Why should they be entitled to have any advantage over you and me?

In fairness to the market makers, it would be a good idea to ensure that the virtual specialist's order book remained anonymous at all times. This would be very similar to the way the ECNs are structured right now. If Morgan Stanley or First Boston want to accumulate stock, the investing public should not have the right to know who is doing the buying and the selling. This would eliminate the problem the market makers face when day traders jump ahead of them because they see a large institution trying to buy or sell stock.

By listing all of these NASDAQ stocks on a centralized order book, another consequence would be that you would completely eliminate the need for electronic communications networks (ECNs) like Island, Instinet, and Archipelago. The creation of ECNs was revolutionary in putting us on the road to a fairer marketplace. However, they too would become obsolete in this revolution. Why would the need for them be eliminated? Because customer orders would be reflected in the marketplace directly, so you wouldn't need to rely upon Island, Instinet, or Archipelago as a vehicle for getting your order displayed.

In addition, because this virtual specialist system would be centralized, you would eliminate a large part of the volatility that we see today. Supply and demand would always be in balance. Why would it be in balance? Because there would be no competing markets, and this would eliminate the fragmentation that we sometimes see. In other words, you would not have stock changing hands at two different price levels at the same time *because all buy and sell orders would be handled on the same order book from the same location.* Remember the example of MP3, which was trading at 104 and at 92 at the same time? In this day and age of technology, how is it fair that these kinds of things are allowed to go on? Keep in mind that you and I are the ones who lose when they are.

Once we completely got rid of the market-maker system, and went to a virtual specialist system, the second change that must take place would be to force the specialist to open his books to the general public. This would be the final wall that would come down. Why are we not allowed to see the depth of the market? Why does the specialist conceal that from us? You have seen in this book how dangerous and unfair it can be for us to trade a stock when the specialist hides the true supply and demand from us. Why does he do that? Because he wants to preserve the status quo, and thus keep his trading edge. Otherwise he would not be able to make a living.

If the specialist was required to open his books, the investing public would be able to see everything that he sees. Is there buying support below the market? Is there a large seller above the market? You would not see who is doing the buying and selling, but you would see the price and how many shares could be bought. Imagine how much easier and less risky it would be to trade stocks this way if we had this information.

THE VIRTUAL SPECIALIST'S ORDER BOOK

The level playing field would be a system that, like the NASDAQ, shows you the depth of the market but, like the NYSE, keeps the market fair and orderly under the supervision of a specialist.

IBM

Buyers		Sellers	
1	$111\frac{1}{8}$	26	$111\frac{1}{4}$
4	$111\frac{1}{16}$	20	$111\frac{5}{16}$
27	$110\frac{7}{8}$	22	$111\frac{3}{8}$
32	$110\frac{3}{4}$	1	$111\frac{7}{16}$

This order book would be both centralized and anonymous. This would ensure that all buyers and sellers, whether large financial institutions or day traders, would be able to see the same supply and demand information at all times, and would also get the best possible price.

In addition, like the NASDAQ system today, the handling of customer orders could be done electronically, so this would eliminate the need for the "floor" as we know it. Also, like the present NYSE system, you could award the duty of specialist in each stock to the firm with the cleanest trading record and thus the highest level of integrity.

Trading in Decimals

There is a very good chance that, by the time this book reaches book stores, we will be very close to moving stock trading into decimals instead of fractions. I am very excited by this prospect because it will allow day traders much more leeway in this game of making profits. Imagine that a stock now trading in a tight $\frac{1}{16}$-point spread goes to decimals. It could trade in a 3-cent bid-ask spread, or it could trade in a 9-cent bid-ask spread. If spreads became too narrow, it would drive speculators away and the spreads would widen again. And once spreads became too wide, it would draw day traders back in. In other words, *it would trade wherever supply and demand dictated.* This would create new opportunities for profit for the day trader.

The Future Is Bright for Day Traders

I look forward to the future because I know that these kinds of changes are inevitable. The "old guard" on Wall Street will do everything in their power to prevent them from happening, but it will only be a matter of time before the floodgates are truly opened. When this happens, two things will occur: Many of the traditional Wall Street jobs will become obsolete and, finally, the day trader will be able to compete fairly with the larger players in the marketplace. And, as a result, the majority of day traders will probably be making money instead of losing it.

So this marks the end of yet another journey. If there is one thing I can leave you with, it is that although there is no such thing as easy money, there has never been a better opportunity than now to exploit these markets for profit. The future looks very bright for day traders. And although the landscape of Wall Street is changing drastically, some things will never change: Fear and greed rule the markets, every buyer has a seller, and every trade has a "sucker." Good luck, and may the gods of trading be with you.

Index

specialist system of. *See* Specialist
system, NYSE
NYSE. *See* New York Stock Exchange

Olde, 69
Online brokerage firms, 49–60, 178
    dirty secrets of, 49–60
    mishandling customer orders, 56–60
    undercutting the specialist, 55–56
    use of market orders by, 52–59
    using, 123–24
Opening a stock, 217–18
Order-handling rules, 35, 150–51
Overshooting the market, 155

Partial fills, 184–85
Patience, importance of, 182
Paying-through the market, 47–48
Payment for order flow, 53–54
Pinning the market strategy, 205–6
Price improvement strategy, 223
Price manipulation
    on the NASDAQ, 91–115, 117–31
    on the NYSE, 187–95
Price movement, 15–16
Procter & Gamble, 154, 155–56, 157
Prudential (PRUS), 26, 69, 70

Quotes, trusting, 115, 122–23, 148–49
Quote screens. *See* NASDAQ Level II
    quote screen

Razor-thin profits, in scalp trading,
    145–74

Salomon Smith Barney (SBSH), 26, 68,
    69, 70
S&P futures, 63–64, 75
Scalp traders, 31–32, 145–74, 175–85
    versus momentum traders, 35, 46,
    146–47, 151
Shorting on downticks, 129–30
Slingshot effect, 63, 82–83
Software, trading, 239
Specialist system, NYSE, 22–25, 27–28,
    152–57, 197–210
    beating the, 211–25
    bluffing by the, 214–16
    price manipulation on, 187–95

Spoofing the market, 126–29, 136–37
Spus call, 64
Stealth bids. *See* Hidden orders
Stock(s)
    illiquid, 175–85
    initial public offerings, 21–22, 85–86
    large-cap, 152
    lopsided, 34
    low-priced, 159–60
    low-volatility, 177
    low-volume, 177
    on NASDAQ, 22, 37–39
    on NYSE, 22, 151–52 157–58,
    159–60
    splits, 42–43
    thin versus thick, 37–45
    worth of, 17
Stock exchanges. *See* NASDAQ; New
    York Stock Exchange
Supply and demand information
    cracks in, 87–89, 199
    on NASDAQ, 29–30, 113–14,
    118–22
    on NYSE, 27–29, 189–95, 218–21
Suretrade (online broker), 50, 178

Thick stocks, 37–45
Thin stocks, 37–45
Trade commissions, 64–65, 159
    on partial fills, 184
Trading strategies, in momentum trading
    applying, 133–44
    backing away from the quoted market,
    110–14
    bear raids, 130–31
    bluffing, 94–95, 96
    buying on a pullback, 133
    dangling the carrot, 97–98, 102
    determining an entry point, 138–39
    hidden orders, 103, 118–22, 124,
    133
    illegal, 110, 128–31
    manipulating stock prices, 91–115,
    117–31
    selecting a stock, 140–41
    selling a large block of stock,
    143–44
    shorting on downticks, 129–30
    spoofing, 126–29, 136–37

FARRELLTRADING.COM

Beat Wall Street at Its Own Game

I offer several products and services to start you on the road to profitable trading.

1. The Day Trader's Survival Guide Video Companion—$199

Two one-hour videos to help you apply the cutting-edge trading strategies in this book, including: NYSE/NASDAQ—Scalping, Momentum Trading, Arbitrage, Manipulating the Markets, Day Trader's Quiz, Dirty Secrets of the Online Brokers

2. The Day Trader's Survival Guide Workshops—$999 and $2,999

Come to our one- and three-day workshops in New York City and other locations around the country, including Southern California. Visit my website for dates and to make reservations.

3. "The Arbitrageur" Virtual Trading Floor—$99 per month

Take a seat next to me on my virtual trading floor. Learn what stocks the top traders are trading, when they are trading them, and why. Updated several times throughout the trading day. NASDAQ, NYSE, and Arbitrage Strategies included. Visit farrelltrading.com for more information.

Visit *www.farrelltrading.com* to order online
or place your order toll-free anytime at 1-800-440-2720

Prices include shipping and applicable taxes

All major credit cards accepted